To Fagle St!

Love & Best Wishes to you all.

Tom Hadaway

Tom Hadaway
The Prison Plays

Including Long Shadows co-written with Pauline Hadaway

edited and with an introduction by Val M^c^Lane

ISBN 1 873757 10 7

First published 2004

Cover Design by Tim Murphy Creative Solutions
Cover Photography Moira Conway MA
Copy-Editor Felicity Hepburn

Published in Great Britain by
The University of Sunderland Press
in association with Business Education Publishers Limited
The Teleport
Doxford International
Sunderland
SR3 3XD

Tel: 0191 5252410
Fax: 0191 5201815

British Cataloguing-in-Publications Data
A catalogue record for this book is available from the British Library

Printed in Great Britain by Athenaeum Press, Gateshead, Tyne & Wear

Contents

Preface

Eighteen years have gone by since the first of these plays was written. During which time the UK prison population has risen by sixty per cent. Children as young as ten may now be held criminally responsible and, under new anti terrorism laws, citizens of this land are being held indefinitely without charge, without trial and without representation. It seems making the world a better place is not achieved through the good intention of a playwright.

Yet these plays were first conceived in response to a voice. Walking the compound of Durham Gaol at the start of my writer's residency, accompanied by a prison officer and David Jenkins, newly elected Bishop of Durham, I volunteered a question:

> Do you think these guided tours help us to discover what is actually happening behind those bars?

At that moment a disembodied voice floated down from the block:

> Me name's Billy. Divven forget it.

The prison officer threw a punitive glare upwards. The Bishop cupped a hand round his ear, as though slightly deaf, and replied to my question:

> There are many ways to discover the truth.

These plays are not mine. They are a response to the *Voices* that opened a channel through prison walls. My thanks to them and to the actors and producers who give them identity.

More good news! Two locations in these prison plays, the H Wing Durham and Nicosia Central Prison are facing closure. However bleak the outlook, there is always room for hope.

Thanks to all those who have been involved in the production of this timely anthology and especially to Val McLane who originated and worked towards its completion. Finally and above all, thanks are due to the prisoners whose experience informs these plays.

Tom Hadaway

Tom Hadaway
The Prison Plays

Including Long Shadows co-written with Pauline Hadaway

Introduction

I first met North East playwright Tom Hadaway in 1974 when he offered his play *The Filleting Machine* to The Live Theatre Company of which I was a founder member. This was the beginning of a fruitful relationship between playwright and company and a lasting friendship between Tom and myself. He is still writing for The Live Theatre, his latest work being a play about Laurel and Hardy to be produced sometime in 2005.

Tom Hadaway began writing seriously for publication when he was over forty years old. Born on Waterville Road in North Shields, he was educated at Ralph Gardner school which he left at fourteen to start work on the Fish Quay. Having had so little formal education, the only book he claims to have read as a child was *David Copperfield*. He claims that he is not a resourceful or literary person yet in his forty year career he has written sixteen stage plays, seven television plays and three screen plays as well as numerous short stories and poems. His first experience of theatre was at the age of twenty-two when he was persuaded by a friend to see a production of Shakespeare's *Cymbeline* and he couldn't understand a word of it. But he loved it, describing it as 'a magical experience'.

His first published work was a short story *called The One That Got Away* which appeared in *The Guardian* newspaper and was read by the playwright Cecil Taylor who was, at that time, based in the North East. Cecil encouraged Tom to write plays even though his first*, A Quaker in Cullercoats*, written in 1972, was described by the *Newcastle Journal* theatre critic Stanley Hurwitz as:

> nothing but a basket of herrings. Hadaway is attempting to paint with oils when he has not yet mastered crayons.

Cecil advised Tom to 'write what you know' and he has taken this advice and capitalised upon it. Tom writes from the heart. He has written about his own background and his family, in for example *God Bless Thee Jackie Maddison,* a play about North East fishing and mining traditions. He has also written about many of the contemporary issues affecting the area such as the loss of traditional industries, community dispersal and changing family values as in *The Filleting Machine, Time and Money, The Low Street* and *The Long Line.* He wrote about immigrant communities based on Tyneside in *The Man From Barbados, Uncle Sanghi* and *Alice and Yusuf.*

In 1986 Tom spent three days a week for twelve weeks, working as a writer in residence in H. M. Prisons of Durham, Frankland and Low Newton. During that time, he encouraged prisoners to write short stories and poems for a booklet called *Prison Writers* published by Iron Press in the same year, comprising a selection of their work interspersed with his own comments. He was deeply affected by the experience, commenting that 'their schooldays are not unlike a prison sentence, and the fault, they are told, lies within themselves.'[1] In 1987 he wrote *Yesterday's Children,* a play about his encounters with the prisoners, many of them women, in the secure 'H' wing of Durham prison. He used their personal stories as a basis for the play's dialectic and their idiosyncratic speech patterns to enrich its dialogue. He was particularly interested in the stories of two women sentenced for terrorist activities: Judith Ward, given a life sentence for alleged IRA activities and Khloud Moughrabi, a Palestinian sentenced to life for terrorism. In 1991 he and his daughter Pauline wrote *Long Shadows* about the Palestinian/Israeli conflict. Here again he was thorough in his research, travelling to Algeria and Cyprus in search of experiential knowledge of the events which form the background to this play. These are the two full-length plays included in this book.

The two one act plays are both based on characters that he adapted from the female prisoners whom he met in Durham. *The Vicious Circle*, written in 1999, is about a prison visit by the aunt of Bridget, another of the long-term prisoners in 'H' wing. *Postcard from God,* written in 2000, is a monologue based on the experiences of Judith

[1] Hadaway, T. (1986) *Prison Writers: An Anthology,* North Shields, Iron Press.

Ward, who spent eighteen years in Durham prison for terrorism before she was released on evidence which proved her innocence.

Yesterday's Children (1987) is written in an episodic, cinematic style with short, self-contained scenes linked by a narrator (Harry) and pithy, earthy dialogue based on his recorded conversations with the actual prisoners. In his stage directions, Tom insists that the all-seeing eye of the prison monitors should be ever present on set, giving poignancy to the prisoners' subjugation and lack of privacy. He expresses his own frustration at the limitations of his task as a prison tutor through the character of Harry who comments on the prison system through his discussions with George, the liberal-minded Assistant Governor. There is much dark humour in the play, not least the abbreviation of the Governor's title to G.O.D. and much of the dialogue is comic and 'in yer face'.

Issues which dominate are: the inhumanity of the prison system, the nature of innocence, the value of punishment, recidivism and 'judicial unfairness'. Harry struggles to understand the nature of terrorism in dialogue with Janet, the IRA activist sentenced to life imprisonment for what is called a 'crime of association'. But he acknowledges the hope expressed in the creativity of the prisoners' own writing and their growing awareness of its therapeutic value. So much so that he is disinclined to leave at the end of his paid tenure and continues to visit voluntarily until forced to leave by the authorities for not 'sticking to the rules'.

The male prisoners are portrayed either as brutalised and angry, animal-like in their behaviour or as saddened recidivists who cannot exist beyond the prison walls. In his introduction to *Prison Writers: An Anthology* he wrote:

> Filled with reproach and rejection… they acquire a massive
> lack of confidence.
> The gutsy ones might run away, the weak slide into
> self-abnegation.
> 'There is no point in our writing anything.'

> Now prison adds to the tattooed, young man's conviction of
> his own worthlessness.
> Open that door, in twelve weeks![2]

The women are seen primarily as pathetic victims of the legal system, stripped of their individuality and unable to cope without medication. Their crimes appear to have been motivated by male domination: social or domestic. Only Janet seems able to survive intellectually and he gives her the penultimate speech via her poem:

> What compels our loving,
> Makes victims of us all.
> But for an act of cruelty
> A bewildered people
> Have walled me up
> With yesterday's children.
> Knowing no other way
> Of repudiating…
> Madness!

(There was also a 60-minute Radio version of the play, renamed *The Prison Writer* and produced by BBC Radio 4 in 1988.)

Long Shadows, (1991) is a theatrical investigation into the realities of the Arab/Israeli conflict. Originally intended to be a story about Ian Davison, the convicted PLO terrorist from South Shields, the play's emphasis changed after Tom and Pauline met Dr. Swee Chai Ang, the writer of *From Beirut to Jerusalem*[3] Tom said of Dr. Ang:

> Hers is a real testimony, not a part of a polemic or political debate. It is a personal experience of a human being, who is not Arab or Israeli, who was there following the massacres in the camps. She brought home to us the ruin of so many people, the colossal tragedy of it all. She made us think how unimportant our play was in comparison.

---

[2] Hadaway, T., ibid.

[3] Ang, Swee Chai, (1989) *From Beirut to Jerusalem*, UK, Grafton Press.

As a result of this meeting, Tom and Pauline changed the thrust of their story. They interwove details from Ian Davison's story with those of Khloud Moughrabi and other Palestinians whom they had met on their travels to Cyprus and Algeria. Tom describes the play as 'a story of people caught up in massive historical events over which they have no control'.

The style is again cinematic, beginning with an ominous dialogue between Jan, a journalist, and the character known only as Sinister Man, with various flashbacks to convey the storyline. A conversation with a PLO terrorist Alec leads to the presentation of a forbidden love story between the Israeli soldier David and the Arab student Khloud, interwoven with alternate scenes of domesticity and violence and ending in catastrophe. The horror of the situation is evidenced by the dramatic change in Khloud brought about by her family's shocking experiences. Tom uses a line from *Yesterday's Children* in the opening scene of the play: 'Real understanding only comes from direct experience' and this play continues his investigation into the issues surrounding terrorist actions which he began in the previous play.

The Vicious Circle (1999) is a continuation of the Bridget McLeod story from *Yesterday's Children.* Separated from her mother as a child, she has been in care all of her life and, after thieving and making escape bids, she ends up in Durham prison where her aunt, Mrs Donachie, an Irish traveller, visits for the first time. However, Bridget is heavily sedated and the visit is not a success.

In this play, Tom returns to the themes of social deprivation and depersonalisation. The play is set in the visiting room of 'H' wing. Tom is meticulous in his description of the physical confines of the prison: 'The visiting room is two cells knocked into one (8' x 12').' The Senior Prison Officer Janine has a humane attitude to her charges, and Mrs Donachie is a comic character in the midst of the claustrophobic depression of the prison. Her language is colourful and colloquial:

> 'H' wing! And don't the' say it's more secure than a duck's bum? An' that's watertight.

She also uses the joke of the Governor's nickname, 'God'.

Mrs Donachie: 'God' spoke to me

S.P.O. Janine: Pardon? Who spoke to you?

Mrs Donachie: 'God'! Himself!

S.P.O. Janine: How did you know it was God?

Mrs Donachie: Wasn't he surrounded by all these important people. All of them givin' it the Yes sir! No sir! Three bags full sir!

This is in sharp contrast to the appearance of her niece Bridget who can only manage a 'thin smile of recognition/pleasure' and cries for her children. She horrifies her aunt by suggesting that she regrets attacking Myra Hindley and has to be physically hauled away by the prison officers for grappling with Mrs Donachie over a holy picture. The play is a sad indictment of the treatment of female prisoners, especially those who are separated from their children.

Commenting on the rising female prison population, in 2003 Juliet Lyon, Director of the Prison Reform Trust, said:

> Women prisoners are trapped in a vicious circle of crime... It is a crime in itself that last year nearly thirteen thousand women went to prison and, of those who were released, a third were homeless, most were in debt, many had lost contact with their families and very few received the help they needed to stay off drugs.[4]

Postcard From God (2000) returns to the situation of Judith Ward, imprisoned for eighteen years for suspected IRA activities then released on crucial new evidence which vindicated her. Tom presents her this time in the character of Judy, a woman in her fifties, who has been asked to speak to the Criminal Cases Review Commission on the subject of miscarriages of justice. The play is a monologue within which Judy talks to the sender of the postcard request, the Governor of Durham prison, where she spent sixteen years on 'H' wing. Again the playwright utilises the information

[4] Extract from an article in *ConVerse*. Manchester, MLA Press, Dec 8, 2003.

gleaned from his research in 1987, but this time we are made more aware of Judy's creative intelligence and her interest in poetry. She quotes Wordsworth and Oscar Wilde and refers to the words of C. P. Taylor, Tom's mentor. Durham and its cathedral are prominent in her thoughts as she talks of her first days of freedom:

> I did in fact get up ti Durham town on the day ya suggested. An' sunny it was, like on ya picture postcard.
>
> There it lay below us. Built on its green hills. Ya other Jerusalem. Holdin' out its bright arms. Castle! Bridges! Parks! Markets! With all ya Geordie folk goin' about their lives. An' above it all that great Cathedral. Crownin' the set! Ya Eternal City 'God'! Before me eyes.

The tone of the dialogue is conversational: she speaks to 'God' as a friend. 'It was ya belief in innocence that won me.' Although the same stories are included here as in *Yesterday's Children* and *The Vicious Circle* for example Bridget's life, the failed suicide attempt with the light flex, the teddy bear tale and the reference to Myra Hindley, the style is altogether more poetic than that of the previous plays:

> Oh an' bring ya Commissioners. Robed in their good
> intention. But let them wear grey suits the better they stand
> like shadows. For sorrow has made holy ground of that
> Durham gaol where laughter would seem profane.
> Remembering those before us, gathered under that pale and
> artificial light, bones brittle with impotence.

In all of his plays Tom Hadaway works carefully and meticulously to construct dialogue. He writes and rewrites until he is satisfied with his finished product and he knows every line of every play. These prison plays are full of real-life, gritty dialogue (including much swearing to reflect the inarticulate speech of the uneducated prisoners) yet they also have a poetic rhythm and musical quality in the language. In *Yesterday's Children,* for example, Harry, the writer, says 'But above me hope gathered on the lintels like the gossip of starlings' and in *The Vicious Circle* Mrs Donachie says of her niece:

> Ye've ti understand, Bridget is a sunshine girl. Used ti the open air an' starry skies. Ti the wild grass an' moorland spaces. If a girl like that sees a ladder, isn't it a stairway ti the stars?

It is a 'crime' in my opinion, that Tom Hadaway has not gained universal recognition for his deeply moving and substantial life's work. While he has been nationally neglected, North East playwrights and theatre companies have lauded his plays, not least Peter Mortimer of Iron Press who has published two Hadaway anthologies[5.] In recognition of Tom's desire to see 'judicial fairness' which he expresses so cogently in these plays, I will end with a quotation from the final play in this collection, *Postcard from God*:

> Are ya listenin' God? This is not ti plead for mercy for the rejected. Or ti call on ya pity for them at the bottom o' the heap. But to cry Justice for the Child! Justice for those not yet born! Ti' break this cycle!

Val M^c^Lane
University of Sunderland

---

[5] Hadaway, T. (1986) *Prison Writers: An Anthology,* North Shields, Iron Press.
Hadaway, T. (1994) *The Long Line,* North Shields, Iron Press.

Yesterday's Children

Tom Hadaway

This play was first performed in a collaboration between The Tyne Theatre Company and Live Theatre on stage at The Live Theatre, Newcastle in November 1987.

Original Cast

Stephen Hancock	Harry
Mike Elliot	Assistant Governor
Mark Elstob	Nicholson, Saunders, 7527, Male Prison Officer, Security Chief
Sammy Johnson	MacDonald, Prisoner in the rain, Male Prison Officer
Brendan Healy	O'Malley, Ackroyd, Albert, Male Prison Officer
Elizabeth Carling	Maria, Sandra, Sharon, Ginger, Female Prison Officer
Denise Welch	Jordan, Marty, Myra, Female Prison Officer
Anne Orwin	Mrs Gates, Bridget, Mam, Pat, Female Prison officer
Eve Bland	Janet

Directed by Max Roberts

Characters

HARRY	Writer-in-Residence
ASSISTANT GOVERNOR (A.G.)	
JANET	IRA Prisoner
SECURITY CHIEF (S.C.)	
MALE PRISON OFFICER (M.P.O.)	
FEMALE PRISON OFFICER (F.P.O.)	
MAM	Janet's Mother
MRS GATES	Resident Teacher

Male Prisoners
NICHOLSON
SAUNDERS
7527
MACDONALD
O'MALLEY
ACKROYD
ALBERT
PRISONER IN THE RAIN

Female Prisoners
MARIA
SANDRA
SHARON
GINGER
BRIDGET
PAT
JORDAN
MARTY
MYRA

Act One

The Apron Stage

Monitor(s): Blank.

HARRY — [*To the audience*] Maybe since the death of Cecil Taylor! You know! The mediocrity of Northern writing.

So the Arts Council were thinking… Writers! They must be locked up somewhere.

As simple as that…

◆ ◆ ◆ ◆ ◆

Assistant Governor's Office

Monitor(s): Prison exterior.

Light up: A.G.'s office M.P.O. present.

A.G. — What we don't want is any bloody celebration of terrorists…

M.P.O. — Sir! [*Collects file. Exits*]

HARRY — [*To the audience*] Couldn't have been what they had in mind… I mean, the only thing Northern Arts have in common with the PLO is wondering if next year they'll still have a roof over their heads.

Me! I hadn't a clue. Never been in a place like this. But 'God' spoke to me.

I had this talk with 'God'…

Well! That's how he signs himself. G.O.D. Governor of Durham. [*Walks into the A.G.'s office*]

HARRY [*Cont'd to the audience*] Three different prisons, male, and female wings, and they came seventeen to seventy from Guatemala to Gateshead…

'It's a matter of balance', 'God' said, 'Get it right.'

'God' knows!

But he has some very civilised A.G.'s… Assistant Governors!

[*Moves to the A.G. Backward glance*] Some!

A.G. I mean I welcome you here! Harry isn't it? I'm George!

It's about time these closed places were opened up. I'm for it! Outsiders, people like yourself coming in. I've nothing to hide. Nothing to be ashamed of. Alright, so some things aren't perfect. I'd freely admit that, but we are trying to do something about it.

I didn't build this place. It's inherited.

Tea… or coffee?

Then I believe they want you in Security… Home Office rules, I.D. Official Secrets Act…

HARRY Oh!

Fade out: A.G.'s Office.

◆ ◆ ◆ ◆ ◆

Security

Monitor(s): A dog becomes very agitated. An M.P.O. holds him in check. Alsatian, face snarling out from the screen.

Light up: The S.C. consults his watch. HARRY is late. Mug shots of prisoners on a wall chart. HARRY joins him.

Monitor(s): The dog relaxes. A general prison view. The M.P.O. moves across it.

HARRY	Sorry!
S.C.	In a prison yard, sir! Always keep an even pace… Don't move too fast… the dogs are trained to take out fast runners…
HARRY	Oh!
S.C.	[*Offers HARRY a key on a chain*] You may wonder why there is a chain attached to this key… Hmmm!
HARRY	So I don't lose it?
S.C.	[*Registers professional dismay*] You will attach it to some secure part of your person… like your belt.
HARRY	I haven't…
S.C.	A belt sir…
HARRY	Not wearing…
S.C.	Is an essential article of dress.
HARRY	Yes!

S.C. The idea of the chain, is to ensure that when the key is taken to the cupboard to remove the books contained therein… You go with it!

HARRY Oh yes!

S.C. Otherwise to prevent malicious, and evil bastards offering to do it for you…

HARRY I see…

S.C. 'Allow me to get your books sir'… No floggin' way sir. They are in constant ferment of diabolical scheming. Do not allow them close enough to read the key number, or it will be whispered into the ear-hole of their evil visitors.

[*Phone rings*] Security! Yes! He's what? Where? Who? [*The S.C. becomes agitated*] Well get his bloody name man! Get his bloody name… [*Rings off*]

Sorry about that Mister…

HARRY Harry!

S.C. What exactly are you here for sir?

HARRY To encourage creative writing…

S.C. Education! I have a lot of respect for it. But I often wonder if it isn't wasted on some. So what exactly would you be looking for?

HARRY I don't really know?

S.C. You don't know?

HARRY Well, you know how it is?

S.C. No!

Monitor(s): Long corridors. M.P.O.s walk in and out of the screen.

HARRY Well! Until something actually appears you cannot really say what it is you might discover… Then when it shows up, you can say, 'There! That's it, that's what I was looking for…'

S.C. I'm not sure that I follow that sir…

HARRY Perhaps it's not the way you work…

S.C. Do you know how long it would take my sniffer dogs to discover a gun?

HARRY I've no idea… er… an hour… a day?

S.C. A week! A floggin' week! Because my sniffer dogs cannot sniff into a metal cupboard, the key of which has been left lying around by some floggin' civilian, who did not know what was happening until it floggin' well happened…

HARRY Oh!

S.C. What would you do sir? Just supposing! Only supposing! Before you left home to come here, and there was a knock on your door, and there was a man stood there who said, 'Take this gun into the education block of prison hex, hex, hex, and on your return, if you have carried out our instruction, you will find your wife, and family in the best of health.'

Hmmm! Eh! What would you say?

HARRY I'm not sure…

S.C. Ah!

HARRY Er! I'd say… I'm not married… I'm single…

Fade out: S.C.

◆ ◆ ◆ ◆ ◆

Assistant Governor's Office

Monitor(s): Empty corridors.

Light up: HARRY returns to A.G.

A.G. You'd be lying of course…

HARRY Of course!

A.G. You have a family Harry! I have a family! Prison officers have families! It's in the back of our minds. Protecting our family!

HARRY I'm not up to life-and-death decisions! Not everyday! My wife's practical.

[*Light up: A prisoner hooded against the rain. Slouching round in a circle. His exercising circle is a cage twelve feet in diameter*]

Monitor(s): M.P.O. and dog stand in the rain.

A.G. You may hear, and see things that seem disturbing…

[*The prisoner begins to circle in his cage*]

Remember you are in a position of trust Harry. We are relying on your discretion. Perhaps you have the public ear. I suggest you are never tempted.

HARRY — In what way?

A.G. — Revelations to the media…

HARRY — You have my word on that…

A.G. — Yes! Well in a way we are placing ourselves in your hands… but I tell you this. If you ever do, it will certainly result in an end to this kind of experiment. It would set the clock back.

The uniformed staff have a difficult job, you must understand that, they've got their hands full… but one thing they can do, believe me! They can close these gates faster than I can.

Fade out: A.G.'s Office.

◆ ◆ ◆ ◆ ◆

Male Wing

Light up: M.P.O.

M.P.O. — First time on the wing sir?

HARRY — Yes!

[*They walk past the prisoner circling in his cage. HARRY pauses in front*]

M.P.O. Shouldn't worry about him. Naughty boy. Rule 43. Has to be exercised on his own. Don't let it upset you. He's an animal!

[*They enter the wing. M.P.O. shakes out his umbrella*]

Monitor(s): Cell block interior.

M.P.O. The net between the landing prevents any harm coming to those inmates who accidentally fall over the rail… [*Pauses*] The door is three quarter steel. The card denotes the inmate… The name… O'Malley! His category… 'A' Sentence, twenty five years…

HARRY Twenty five years?

M.P.O. Have you seen in a cell yet sir?

HARRY Not yet…

[*M.P.O. unlocks O'MALLEY'S cell. Light up: A giant bearded man occupies the threshold*]

M.P.O. Alright O'Malley… just showing him your cell…

O'MALLEY [*Snarling*] Eh! It's no' ma fuckin' cell! It's your fuckin' cell, an' ye can have the fuckin' thing back as soon as ye want.

[*M.P.O. retreats behind HARRY*]

As for you! [*Jerking a finger at HARRY*] Don't you believe all they fuckin' tell ye. An' don't poke yor fuckin' nose in here. [*He slams his door shut*]

M.P.O. — The doors are self-locking. There are fourteen cells on this landing proceeding in an elliptical form…

HARRY — [*To the closed door*] Sorry!

M.P.O. — Not like your ordinary criminal. Considers himself a prisoner of war…

Fade out: Male Wing.

◆ ◆ ◆ ◆ ◆

The Cathedral Close

Monitor(s): The Cathedral Close, closing to the cathedral.

Light up: A.G. and HARRY.

A.G. — If we cut through the close, there's a very good restaurant next to the cathedral. And I want to take some pictures for my son. He's an architect.

So, how did you get on?

HARRY — Frightening!

A.G. — I mean what did you think of the cell?

HARRY — Never saw it yet. All I saw was the beard and the wild eyes. I mean I felt a right in-between. You don't think they wanted that?

A.G. — The shock confrontation! O'Malley! Big isn't he?

HARRY — Monumental!

A.G. There you are then. You see what they've got on their hands?

HARRY Bloody hell! The anger! The defiance! Shut the door himself! Shut us out!

A.G. [*Hands HARRY a note*] From the remand wing. Request. Your first client! She's on quite a serious charge. [*Walks on*]

HARRY [*Pauses to read*] George!

A.G. Yes.

HARRY Are we insured?

Fade out: Cathedral Close.

◆ ◆ ◆ ◆ ◆

Remand Wing

Monitor(s): Women inmates in a prison workroom. F.P.O. comes through the screen.

Light up: F.P.O., HARRY and JORDAN.

F.P.O. This way sir!

[*Opens a cell. Female prisoner JORDAN, attractively dressed, middle class, seated. HARRY enters. JORDAN rises. F.P.O. enters, reads from order form*]

Remand prisoner D25730 Jordan! Request… Visiting tutor! Thirty minutes sir…

HARRY Thank you!

[*F.P.O. leaves. HARRY surprised*]

JORDAN — It's alright! Remand prisoners are allowed private interviews.

Monitor(s): F.P.O. watching. Full face.

HARRY — Oh! Well my name is…

JORDAN — Do I look like the sort of woman who would murder her husband?

HARRY — Pardon?

JORDAN — Just look at me! Do I give you that impression?

HARRY — Er! No! Not really…

JORDAN — So you feel quite safe in here with me?

HARRY — Well… yes! Of course!

JORDAN — You can always press the alarm. [*She smoothes down her skirt*] Appearances are very important aren't they?

HARRY — Oh! They can be… important…

JORDAN — My solicitor says it's vital I create a good impression…

HARRY — Yes! [*Notices a photograph*] Your children?

JORDAN — Margaret is nine, Pauline five… I've told them I'm working for the Government… Scrubbing these floors… I suppose in a way I am…

Oh, you wouldn't believe what has happened to me… Oh, and the lies! My God, the lies! I want to tell everyone the truth... Look, I want to write my life story... How should I begin...?

HARRY — Well... How about... '"Do I look like the sort of woman who would murder her husband?" She said, by way of reassurance...' Sorry!

JORDAN — It's what they are saying... Do you know what we had? One hundred and twenty bedrooms! Seventeen acres, paddocks, heated swimming pool. The largest hotel in North Riding... A yacht in Marbella! So you think I'd deprive my children of a father who gave us all that...? [*Agitatedly lighting a cigarette*] I was educated at Roedean! I'm allowed privacy here... I can't bear to mix with those other women. I'm not used to people like that. Some of them are dreadful... Oh yes, I fell in love with another man! Is that so terrible? A love affair! People just fall in love all the time, don't they? What's unusual about that? But the lies! Oh God the lies!

HARRY — Roedean! The girl's public school! Brighton?

JORDAN — Yes! *Very* select...

HARRY — Of course! And your husband, does... did he come from Brighton?

JORDAN — [*Pause*] Doncaster! [*Unable to conceal a note of revulsion*]

Fade out: Remand Wing.

Monitor(s): Empty corridors/cell block.

◆ ◆ ◆ ◆ ◆

Pub

Monitor(s): Blank.

Light up: A.G. and HARRY.

A.G. [*Handing HARRY a pint*] So you've had your look round?

HARRY Thanks. Yes, I was hoping to push it a stage further…

A.G. The Governor is with you. Very happy!

HARRY Good! If we could move more freely…

A.G. It's the Governors of prisons Harry who are in the forefront of change, in the battle for reform… They have to administer this over-crowding. This Victorian set up, and it's no good to them…

[*Enter MRS GATES*]

Ah Mrs Gates! This is Harry!

[*She nods slightly. Remains standing*]

Mrs Gates is a resident teacher on the female wing. Anything they write. We'd appreciate it if you'd channel it through her… yes… excuse me. [*He exits*]

HARRY Ah! What subjects do you cover?

MRS GATES General.

Monitor(s): The A.G. Full face.

HARRY So, you'll be very familiar with what's going on?

MRS GATES Sorry.

HARRY I mean how do you find it? Are the women responsive?

MRS GATES It varies.

HARRY Amazing eh! In the middle of all these men. Thirty six aren't there? Cameras! Electronic doors! That great razor wire fence. Keeps the men out does it?

MRS GATES Pardon?

HARRY But in prison, I suppose you have your own services eh! Education! Medical! Welfare! Chaplain! Like a great village eh? People like me wandering in off the street. Bit of an intrusion eh? So what level do you take them to?

MRS GATES O-U.

HARRY O-U. Really? Well there's something eh! Yes! Hmmm. Well! [*Confidentially*] Bit of tension in these places don't you think?

MRS GATES Pardon.

HARRY Personally I put it down to the plumbing. Do they still slop out on the women's wing? Degrading eh? Well, as it is for the men. Wouldn't you think the least amenity to give a human being would be a flush toilet?

MRS GATES Ssssh!

HARRY Sorry?

MRS GATES Ssssh!

HARRY Ssssh?

Monitor(s): Empty corridor.

A.G. [*Returning*] There you are [*Gives Mrs Gates a file*]

MRS GATES Thank you A.G. Well! It's lovely to have had a chat, and really nice to have met you Mr. er…

HARRY Ssssh!

[*Mrs Gates exits*]

A.G [*Looking up*] I think they are planning something for you Harry…

HARRY Oh!

A.G. On the male wing… Cheers! You've asked for an audience…

HARRY Well, I thought if I could meet a number together, I'd get the message over…

A.G. Message?

HARRY That I'm here…

A.G. Oh they know you're here. You should be prepared Harry. I tell you frankly, there are some just waiting to see you fail… I mean it's a split. But there are some, who regard your presence as a mistake…

HARRY Oh!

A.G. Nothing personal… But I thought we should have this drink together…

Fade out: Pub.

◆ ◆ ◆ ◆ ◆

Male Wing – Education Room

Monitor(s): Prisoners move through the monitor.

Light up: ACKROYD, MACDONALD.

ACKROYD [*To anyone in the audience*] Hey! My drinkin' mate on the out! Alright Charlie! Back again eh? How's the Ord Arms?

A see you've gorra few bruises eh? Get them on the sheet! Who done you Charlie?

Regional Crime Squad! Bastards! Let ye dee the crime afore the' lift ye…

MACDONALD [*To anyone in the audience*] Hey Paddy! Y'rup on the twos? Knocked ye back did the'? Ye signed for yer T.I.C.s? Give em some decent write-offs man! They'll put a word in to the parole board,

ACKROYD Yeh! Tell'm about how ye did all the washin' line nicks in South Gosforth.

MACDONALD Worra divi! What y' doin' on education? Y' what? Decision makin!

Worra divi! Keep off the Holloway jam kidda, it's that thin it slides off the bread.

[*Enter M.P.O.*]

M.P.O. Right you two. On that mark.

[*To audience. Walking through with clipboard*] Smith 2597! Saunders 2643! Anderson 1398! Thompson 2251! [*Two prisoners file into the audience*] MacDonald 4126. Ackroyd 7127. [*They take up a disruptive, and surly stance. Engage the audience*] Right you lot, settle down! Pack it in… [*Picking on anyone in the audience*] No sodden trouble from you, right! And you, keep your bum on that seat. And you… and you…

ACKROYD Hey chief! A wanna do geography for Open University y'knaa!

M.P.O. What would you want geography for Ackroyd? You ain't goin' no fuckin' where.

MACDONALD A'm not supposed tae be here Boss. A'm on woodwork…

M.P.O. You was on woodwork MacDonald, an' you can crawl back into it later, but right now you are on creative English…

MACDONALD Up the English…

M.P.O. You can tell that to the man when he comes… He wants an audience!… Right! He's got one… You wanna give someone a hard time, here's your chance… But… if it gets out of hand… down that fuckin' block you go… and I mean everyone of you… [*Takes up a seat. Takes out a newspaper*]

[*HARRY advances*]

HARRY Hello!

[*To M.P.O.*] Didn't expect so many…

[*To audience*] Haven't been forced here, have you?

Oh! (You have)…

Anyway… I'm Harry… OK? I wanted to say something about writing… I wanted to tell you… it is only a way of recording experience!

Well, inside each of you… apart from the problems… and I suppose you all have problems… or you wouldn't be here… eh!… I mean any of us…

Locked within each of you, is something unique, and special… the life you've lived… Oh some write better than others. Some on an ego trip… or it's a nice way to earn a living… but writing doesn't belong only to those who do it brilliantly. They can't say… 'keep off the grass'…

ACKROYD Hey Mister! [*Pointing to anyone*] That's Davy Saunders… he's a friggin' grass… ye want ti keep off him.

MACDONALD Tha's right! Tha's right!

Hey Saunders, you are a friggin' grass. You are gonna get the toothbrush up your arse…

HARRY [*Struggling for control*] Anymore… Anymore… than with music, or painting, singing, or dancing…

ACKROYD Oh singin' an' dancin'! Like the theatre! Are wi ganna gerra birra singin', an' dancin'… mister?

HARRY I suppose prison may be like a theatre, in that it's not the answer to anything, but answers may be in there somewhere…

ACKROYD Oh' A like a birra singin' an' dancin'!…

MACDONALD Sorta shits this? Eh? Sorta shit?

HARRY I wanted to tell you, you can take your memories, and you can add to them not only how you felt at the time, but how you feel about them now… You know! Like in an argument, when it's always the next day you think of all the things you could have said… Writing will allow you to do that…

ACKROYD Mister! A divven knaa a full stop from a comma!

MACDONALD Aye! He's only fit fer mixin' batches o' cement. No even a paper hanger! That's why he's such a criminal…

HARRY Oh' it's true… only five per cent of working class lads pass the exams, and come to the cultural inheritance.

[*The M.P.O. for all to see unfolds his newspaper, revealing the headline: 'The Sun.' Then hides behind it*]

For the rest, schooldays filled with reproach, and rejection… are like a prison sentence… 'Are you listening to me boy?' 'You have had your chance, and you have blown it'… Reminded, again, and again through frailty, and weakness, that finally we are to blame for our own failure. Hopes, and dreams are frustrated, and we are left drained of self confidence.

MACDONALD Hey! What y'r on aboot? 'We'... What's all this 'we'?

HARRY I'm playing the gallery...

MACDONALD Had on! Where'd you get you're education?

HARRY Maybe I was one of the lucky ones...

MACDONALD Maybe! Let me tell you where I get mine. The con I share a cell with, he educates me.

HARRY Then you are a victim...

MACDONALD Victim o' what?

HARRY Maybe of society that cares more about property than about people...

MACDONALD [*To ACKROYD*] He's a burglar! He cares mair about property than he does aboot people... You thick or somethin'?

HARRY That's something we could talk about later.

MACDONALD No! We'll talk aboot it now!

ACKROYD Mister! Divven wind him up. He's a nutta...

MACDONALD Up you Geordie! Listen... You! I'm sick o' the shit, 'It's all 'cos o' me upbringin'!' Why pretend tae be inadequate. Don't you identify me wi' losers, right! My crime is a result of rational choice... Crime is the ultimate conclusion of capitalism... right! What di ye do if yor skint?

ACKROYD [*To the audience*] A nicked a crane. Sold it ti Hertz for eighty quid...

MACDONALD Did they get done?

ACKROYD No friggin' way…

MACDONALD Hey! An' yor Matthey Johnstone Bank eh! Yor Guinness directors! Oh aye' they can write. An' add up! They's educated. They sell money! If yor country's money weakens, they flog it for dollars, an' yens. They's given us genuine criminals a bad name. 'Cos they can write…

HARRY And where do you draw the line?

MACDONALD Sorta line?

HARRY Would you go into your neighbour's house? The people you live next to… would you rob your own class?

MACDONALD If they've got the money… why not?

HARRY Old people?

MACDONALD Ooh! Listen tae him… Same old fuckin' story… What aboot the owld folk… The' always bring that oot… Listen! If they've got it all hidden away… Where did they get it from?

HARRY And violence?

MACDONALD Violence! A'm no against violence… A've lived wi' it since a was a wee'n. Violence was done tae me in the pram.

Happiest day in my live, a had a screw in ma cell, an' a beat him tae a pulp, in heap o' shit afore the' could get at me. A'm no against violence…

[*ACKROYD is desperately signalling to HARRY that MACDONALD is crazy*]

Listen Mister! If a ever find oot where you live, an' a pay you a visit, just be glad when A come awa', you are still alive…

M.P.O. [*Up on his feet*] Right! Out! Out!

[*ACKROYD comes forward. Raises his arms. Body search then exits. MACDONALD follows, raises his arms, body search*]

Rest of you! Clear the block! Now!

MACDONALD Nae hard feelin' ye ken… [*Exits*]

M.P.O. Out! Out!

[*To HARRY*] You soft on criminals sir? [*Exits*]

Fade out: Male Wing – Education Room.

◆ ◆ ◆ ◆ ◆

The Cathedral Close

Monitor(s): Durham Cathedral.

O.S. the summons of bells.

Light up: A.G. and HARRY.

A.G. [*Taking camera shots*] Come into the foreground. I'll get a shot of the tower.

HARRY What would you recommend George?

A.G. You only have a few months here... Survive them! Any con would tell you that...

HARRY I can't redress the wasted years... Just... I believe if they made a beginning... Y'know! Picked up a pen, and wrote 'This happened to me', maybe hearts and minds would open up...

A.G. Seems safe enough... good luck!

HARRY Maybe it's just a literacy problem...

A.G. Eh?

HARRY Crime!

A.G. You aren't a Marxist are you Harry? Hold it. That's it.

HARRY I'm not the sort to get politically involved...

A.G. Good! Hold it! My son is an architect. He says Durham cathedral is the finest building in Europe.

HARRY Just there seems a lot of tension. Is there something I don't understand?

A.G. You aren't into religion?

HARRY Hell no!

A.G. Good! Can you imagine the effects of these bells on prisoners?

HARRY Er... Redemption maybe!

A.G. It's a joke...

HARRY Redemption is a joke?

A.G. Crudely put… 'Kick that cripple in the nuts Esmeralda!'

HARRY The what?

A.G. Quasimodo! The Bells! The Bells!

HARRY Oh! What happened to rehabilitation George?

A.G. Whatever they write, will have to be submitted… no taking it away… unapproved…

HARRY I understand…

A.G. We are presiding over a lost generation.

HARRY You think so! But is it doing any good… collecting all these tragic people under one roof?

A.G. [*Relaxes from his camera*] The prison, and this cathedral, are one, and the same stone Harry. They represent an architect's sincere believe in evil. The one to keep it out, the other to keep it in.

HARRY I don't like to think of anyone as lost.

A.G. Don't you! Well, that's good.

HARRY I mean, how do you feel?

A.G. I don't know if I can confide that.

HARRY Do you go along with this idea of evil?

A.G. Well, I more or less have to... I work for the Home Office...

Monitor(s): A barred gate with an approaching F.P.O. and two female prisoners: JANET and BRIDGET. They stop at the screen. Look out. JANET peering round the F.P.O.

A.G. You'll be alright on the women's wing Harry!

[Light up: F.P.O. unlocks JANET and BRIDGETS cell]

I've put the word around. They are expecting you. Some intelligent young women.

HARRY Oh...

A.G. Thirty six women in the middle of one thousand two hundred men... Electronic doors, cameras, high security. There are some who think it's dehumanising! So, there's a campaign by the way, to have it closed. People outside! We'd rather you didn't get involved...

HARRY Of course not.

A.G. Yes... One in particular. Janet! I'd like your opinion.

Monitor(s): Empty corridor.

The Guinness Book of Records mass murderess of Britain...

Fade out: Cathedral Close.

◆ ◆ ◆ ◆ ◆

Female Cell

HARRY — I've never really been a success with women. [*Turns to JANET*]

[*Light up: JANET and BRIDGET*]

JANET — Real stories eh?

HARRY — Why not? Could be a revelation!

JANET — Bloody sure!

HARRY — Well?

JANET — The male cons, they shout over to us… you heard 'em? 'Slags!' 'Cows!' 'Show's yor tits!' They make us grub, an' they piss in it… Wimmin in prison is socially rubbish! Who'd listen…? This is Bridget by the way…

HARRY — Hello Bridget…

JANET — She's a puddin'… Aren't ye a puddin'?

BRIDGET — Hi ya!

JANET — Who cares what we got to say?

HARRY — In the end you have each other…

JANET — Who let you in here?

HARRY — You see! Someone opened a door!

JANET — What ye think o' this place then?

Monitor(s): F.P.O. returning to the screen. Followed by MARTY. They halt.

HARRY — Claustrophobic!

JANET — Like a submarine eh! Hey di ye think it's a submarine wirron Bridget?

BRIDGET — Friggin' right!

HARRY — Like the engine room of a ship.

JANET — Yeh! Only the engine has stopped, an' it isn't goin' no where…

HARRY — It's clean. I've been on the male wing.

BRIDGET — What's it like?

HARRY — Well if this is the engine room. They're in the bilges.

JANET — Always come that line. The men's worse off. They're on bed, and breakfast! We're lifers!

HARRY — So how long…?

JANET — Have I been in here! Fourteen years!

Fourteen friggin' years…

HARRY — Christ!

JANET — You was sayin'…?

HARRY — You must be Janet…

JANET — Do you mind… Don't mix me up with that crazy bastard…

HARRY — Sorry!

JANET — Yeh! That bomber! That dangerous looney! Don't you label me with her right!

HARRY — Right!

[*The F.P.O. and MARTY move through the screen*]

Monitor(s) Empty corridor.

But fourteen years…

JANET For shop liftin'…

[*BRIDGET enjoys HARRY being kidded. Light up: MARTY, she saunters over*]

HARRY Shop lifting?

JANET Yeh! But I do a good job. liftin' from one street to the next…

[*The girls enjoy the joke*]

Ah! Sorry! Yeh' yer right! I'm JANET! I'm always takin' the piss. Keeps me sane. This is Marty! Tell the man what ye did Marty, It's confession time…

MARTY Fuck off!

JANET Listen! This is a gentleman come to help improve us image right!

HARRY Well, I may not be a gentleman…

JANET No! Are we in serious moral danger here then?

Fade out: Female Cell.

[*They all laugh raucously*]

[*Light up: Return to Cathedral Close and A.G.*]

A.G. A few flippant remarks, Harry. Are you into conscience, or the correction of grammar?

HARRY Certainly not the correction of grammar.

A.G. What then?

HARRY Their real stories.

A.G. Take it from me. There's no pissing in the grub.

HARRY They fear what they write may be used against them.

A.G. Nonsense.

HARRY Accommodate the fear. Guarantee confidentiality.

A.G. Licence to create mayhem. Cant be done!

HARRY Just have to cope…

A.G. Oh people cope. Somewhere, somehow, out of sight people cope.

Fade out: Cathedral Close and A.G.

◆ ◆ ◆ ◆ ◆

Induction

Light up: Two F.P.O.s, young. MARIA, prisoner, middle-aged. Pile of clothing.

F.P.O.1 Another body for you...

F.P.O.2 Right dear! Name please?

MARIA Maria!

F.P.O.2 C'mon girl! C'mon girl! Maria what?

MARIA Hutching!

F.P.O.2 You got her property cards?

F.P.O.1 Checked!

F.P.O.2 Thank yooo!

F.P.O.1 You and John get out last night?

F.P.O.2 Joking! Time I got home...

F.P.O.1 Know the feeling!

F.P.O.2 Just flopped! 'Your muther's got the kids'. I said, 'She can bloody keep'm.' Men!

F.P.O.1 Is it worth it?

F.P.O.2 Right dear! You are allowed four sets of clothes. You understand that? Four tops, four bottoms, four pairs of shoes. Right! You can have a dress, but it will be classed as a top, and a bottom. Pick out from there what you want!

[*MARIA rummages through the clothes*]

F.P.O.1 Another ten hours today, who's serving the time?

F.P.O.2 That's five. You got five tops there… put it back…

MARIA Pardon?

F.P.O.2 You speak English eh?

MARIA A little!

F.P.O.2 Good! Put it back! That's plain English! Take it off her! Right! Thank yooo! Can we have a list of your jewellery?

F.P.O.1 Can't have jewellery anyway!

F.P.O.2 Thank you madam deputy governor, know-all! I still need a list…

F.P.O.1 Just saying!

F.P.O.2 That ring has a diamond…

F.P.O.1 You can't have any rings with stones in.

F.P.O.2 Take it off…

F.P.O.1 Off! The ring… off!

MARIA Engagement ring…

F.P.O.1 Is it! Take it off! Not allowed! Oh Christ! Take… it… off! Are you going to take that ring off, or do we take it off for you…?

F.P.O.2 Thank yooooo! God! Time is it?

F.P.O.1 [*Yawns*] Dunno! January! February! March! [*Gropes MARIA's hair… ears…*]

MARIA Ouch!

F.P.O.1 No ear-rings!

F.P.O.2 [*Writing*] No ear-rings!

F.P.O.1 One medal! Silver! With chain…

MARIA Please!

F.P.O.2 Religious is it?

F.P.O.1 Yeh! Definitely…

F.P.O.2 Sort of religion? What Ree----li----jin are you?

F.P.O.1 Why are you wearing a religious medal?

MARIA My mother!

F.P.O.1 That don't matter. You can't have it unless you are practising religious.

F.P.O.2 Thank yooo! [*Examines*] Church of England?

F.P.O.1 Naw! Catholic!

F.P.O.2 Don't matter if it's Bhuddist! [*Throws it down*] It's orf…

F.P.O.1 Right!

F.P.O.2 Thank you! Stand over there! On that piece of sheet, and take your clothes off…

[*To F.P.O.1*] Well, I said to him 'You're the one is on about the bloody mortgage and insurance, an' the…'

[*To MARIA*] Look! Over there! Take your clothes off…

MARIA — Please!

F.P.O.2 — Clothes off!

MARIA — No!

F.P.O.1 — What you mean, 'no'? Look we gotta place down there for 'no-no's'. You wanna go in it. Right!

F.P.O.2 — It's a routine strip search dear! Everybody comes in does it…

MARIA — No!

F.P.O.2 — Stand over there, and take your clothes off, or they will be taken off you…

F.P.O.1 — Are you refusing a direct order?

F.P.O.2 — That's it! Call somebody please!

F.P.O.1 — Are you taking your clothes off?

F.P.O.2 — Take the clothes off her…

MARIA — No! No! Get off! Leave me alone…

[*Black*]

◆ ◆ ◆ ◆ ◆

Female Wing – Education Room

Monitor(s): F.P.O.s on surveillance.

Light up: JANET writes. MARTY irons a blouse. BRIDGET reading a letter. They roll the thin cigarettes known as nails. HARRY enters. Puts down his tape recorder.

JANET — It's how it happens Harry. All the tension.

HARRY — New arrival was she?

JANET — Civilisation! Strip us off, an' it's snap… snap! I mean her kid was dead.

MARTY — 'Ungarian in't she Jan?

JANET — Yeh! She's called Maria.

BRIDGET — She's cuttin' up.

JANET — In the strips.

BRIDGET — Yeh! Cuttin' up proper.

HARRY — What's that mean Bridget… cutting up?

BRIDGET — You wanna cut yor wrists, you gotta cut'm up.

MARTY — Yeh! Cuttin' sideways is just attention seekin'…

JANET — It don't work.

BRIDGET — Reportable offence… suicide…

MARTY — Muppet is she?

JANET — Confirms my theory. Victims invite their own fate.

MARTY	In 'Olloway we 'ad a girl in for murder. Weren't the full shillin'. Everyone kept tellin' 'er, 'You got evil eyes'. One night... she gouged 'em out...
HARRY	God Almighty!
MARTY	Yeh! Wiv a plastic knife. Don' know what 'appened to 'er... 'Ere 'arry! You tapin' this? Well, I think they managed to save one of 'em. Yeh! They gotta good 'ospital in 'olloway...
HARRY	How old are you Marty?
MARTY	Comin' up twenty one.
JANET	Hasn't hit her yet. Only been here two years. It'll take another two before she realises...
MARTY	Awright gran'ma...
JANET	So I'm tellin' you. This new girl Maria. She's murdered her seven year old kid. Tried to do herself in at the same time...
BRIDGET	She got thirty six stitches...
MARTY	'Ow you know that? Where you getting' all this information?
BRIDGET	Talkin' to the sister...
MARTY	Oh! got somethin' goin' 'ave we?
BRIDGET	Sister's alright!
MARTY	Alright for some...

BRIDGET You gotta chip on yor shoulder?

MARTY What she tell you for, an' not tell us?

BRIDGET Jealous! 'Cos yor not gettin' medicine.

MARTY Wassup wi' you?

BRIDGET Took you off treatment did she?

[*F.P.O. passes through*]

JANET Watch it…

How do you spell hysterectomy sir?

[*The girls snigger*]

F.P.O. [*Enters*] This the creative writing class is it?

HARRY This is what turned up…

F.P.O. The three horrors!

JANET Aw don' be like that Chiefy.

MARTY Worryin' about yor boyfriend are you Chiefy?

F.P.O. I don't have to worry about my boyfriend…

BRIDGET Yeh! Who's havin' it off with'm tonight Chiefy?

F.P.O. Not you… an' that's for sure!

You have permission for that tape recorder sir?

HARRY From the Governor! I have a letter here… [*Demonstrates the letter*]

F.P.O. Uh huh! Right! You three… watch it! [*Exits*]

JANET Alright that one. Somes got a sense of humour. But they got to have two faces. One for in here, one for when they go home.

HARRY You were saying about Maria.

JANET Yeh! She's had this helluva life with a man.

BRIDGET Wouldn't cha know…

JANET Bastard, beat her up an' that. So she's goin' over the wall, an' takin' her kid at the same time. Seven years she's got. She's sick! Shouldn't be in a place like this.

BRIDGET Nobody's got the right to kill kids…

JANET What you sayin'…

BRIDGET Just sayin'… kids gotta right ti live…

JANET What would you know yor a puddin'… What they never understand about crime Harry, is the circumstances. All you get in court, is what happened. You never get to know the circumstances.

BRIDGET I still say…

JANET Maybe it was all unbearable…

MARTY C'mon you two. Lay off!

BRIDGET Not gettin' at you Jan…

MARTY Look Jan… tell 'arry about Cynthia! Go'on give's a laugh…

BRIDGET Yeh! Tell'm about Cynth...

MARTY C'mon Jan. Give's a laugh.

JANET [*Rising up. Performing*] Yeh! Well she was ill... I mean really ill. Every night she's gonna do herself in. No one takin' a blind bit o' notice... No sympathy from us.

MARTY No way.

JANET I mean, stone me! We got us bird to do. Twenty, thirty years... without copin' with desperately sick people...

MARTY Tha's right.

JANET There she went on... 'I'm gonna kill meself... I'm gonna kill meself.' I'm talkin' about every night y'know, when we's tryin' ti get some sleep...

BRIDGET All day they's pumpin' her full o' drugs.

MARTY But she was comin' out o' them at night, when the rest of us is turnin' in...

JANET 'A wanna die. A wanna die.'

She's in the strips... y'know... just a smock, an' a mattress... No way she can harm herself... 'I'm countin' to ten, then I'm gonna kill meself...' 'For Gawd's sake.' We all shouted back, 'Gerron with it...'

TOGETHER Ten... nine... eight... seven... six... five...

JANET Y'know... if we could've thought of a way to help her...

HARRY Help her?

JANET

Yeh! Help her top herself… Like if you get yor baccy tin, stand on it 'til it's flat, you can get a sharp edge to cut up with… that sorta thing. Anyhow she's got this idea herself. The alarm button! All cells has got'm.

MARTY

Good old Cynth.

JANET

She picks away at the plaster… round the alarm button… to get at the flex… An' it works… She's pickin' away, an pickin' away, an' out comes a little bit o' flex, an' a bit more, an' a bit more… 'til she's got enough ti wrap round her neck… So, with it firmly wrapped round, she shouts, 'Goodbye world,' an' flops onto the floor…

What happens? Another yard o' bloody flex comes out! Picks herself up! Charges across the cell… more bloody flex… Bloody cell's festooned with it. An' all the bloody alarm bells is goin' off. Screws is dashin' round. Reassurin' everybody. Lookin' in the spy holes. 'Everythin's alright Penny, don' get upset.' 'Fault on the system Lorna, don' worry.' Til they come to the strip cell. 'Nothin' to worry about Cynthia… oh' my Gawd…' There she is, sittin' in the middle of all this wirin', an' she's laughin'. Yeh! Laughin'! It struck her as bein' so funny, she's give up any thought of killin' herself.

Fade out: Female Wing – Education Room.

◆ ◆ ◆ ◆ ◆

The Prison Yard

Monitor(s): Prison exterior.

Light up: The A.G. and HARRY walk to the gate.

HARRY — I'm telling you George, the girl's a joker. The way she tells a story.

A.G. — You'd have to ask yourself, would her victims be laughing.

HARRY — Hard to reconcile. Should they have that kind of humour… terrorists?

A.G. — I'd say you are very impressionable Harry. It's a serious defect. Come on. We'll go and have a drink.

Fade out: Prison Yard, A.G. and HARRY.

◆ ◆ ◆ ◆ ◆

Male Cell

Monitor(s): A blank steel door.

Light up: A cell, three–up. ACKROYD crouched on his bunk, a blanket over his head. SAUNDERS lies on his bunk. MACDONALD paces the cell. Three paces in each direction take him to its boundary.

MACDONALD — [*Snatching the blanket off ACKROYD*] What you doin'?

ACKROYD — Savin' me breath. [*Restores the blanket*]

SAUNDERS — Freezin'…

MACDONALD [*Climbs on a chair to look out of the window*] Fuckin' snow. Be no exercise! Stuck threed up in this poxy cell all day.

SAUNDERS Game o' cards Acka?

ACKROYD Nah.

MACDONALD Cards! Who you vote for Saunders?

SAUNDERS Don't vote Macsi!

MACDONALD Why not?

SAUNDERS Just never bother.

MACDONALD Fuckin' apathy that's what.

SAUNDERS Y'reckon?

MACDONALD You know what the major parties stand for?

SAUNDERS One's for the rich an one's for the poor, aint it?

MACDONALD 'Cos of idiots like you we's gonna get sterilised one day. 'Cos them conservatives says we only breeds criminals... Hey, yoo Ackroyd! [*Snatches off the blanket*] I said what ye doin'?

ACKROYD Pack it in Macsi.

MACDONALD You thinkin' o' doin' some writin for that cunt... Are ye? Or are ye thinkin' o' wimmin? What ye doin' Ackroyd?

ACKROYD Knock it off.

MACDONALD You canna even read.

ACKROYD Course I can.

MACDONALD Yeh! What ye read then?

ACKROYD Micky Spillane.

MACDONALD Yeah! He's alright. [*Throws the blanket over ACKROYD*]

SAUNDERS Pigeons is shoutin' on the ledge Macsi! You gonna feed'm?

MACDONALD Poor little bastards. Ma wee friends, an' companions. Starvin'.

SAUNDERS Gorra load o' bread Macsi.

MACDONALD Yeh!

SAUNDERS Took it off the trays this mornin'.

MACDONALD Cap'n Black says we gets nicked for encouragin' them.

SAUNDERS Just a screw Macsi!

MACDONALD He says they's vermin.

SAUNDERS A screw!

MACDONALD Press this button and a cunt will appear. They's no vermin. Course I'm gonna feed'm. They's ma wee friends. You know when a con dies they take his soul on its last journey.

SAUNDERS S'right Macsi?

MACDONALD [*Snatching off the blanket from ACKROYD*] Hey Acka! Yoo could write tae the Animal Liberation Front. 'Man penalised for feedin' birds, durin' bleak snowy weather.'

SAUNDERS That's good Macsi! Heh! Heh!

MACDONALD A remember the time the bastards sent me tae Broadmoor. A was only twenty one.

SAUNDERS What did they do that for Macsi?

MACDONALD 'Cos I battered a screw. Treatin' me like a was a turd. What a place that was... Broadmoor! Might have got tae me, if a didna have a sense of humour!

A went tae the shit-house. This guy was makin' weird noises. A looked over the cubicle. There he was wi' a turd on his heed. A says 'What ye deein'?'

He says 'A'm in the pub havin' a pint.'

'Oh aye?'

'Yes it really works. Ye can transport yersel' anywhere wi' shit on yer napper.'

[*SAUNDERS climbs off his bunk and gets his potty*]

What ye doin' Saunders?

SAUNDERS Need a crap Macsi!

MACDONALD You are not havin' a crap Saunders!

SAUNDERS Got the runs Macsi!

MACDONALD You are not stinkin' this cell out...

SAUNDERS Macsi!

MACDONALD [*Seizing SAUNDERS by the throat*] All fuckin' night! Stuck in here wi' your stinkin shit… no way!

SAUNDERS Macsi…

MACDONALD I'm gonna plug yor arse. Get your kecks off! [*Releases SAUNDERS. SAUNDERS cringes into a corner*]

SAUNDERS No! No Macsi! No! Please!

MACDONALD Come here! [*Closes on SAUNDERS*]

SAUNDERS No! No! [*Screams*]

[*ACKROYD puts the blanket over his head*]

Fade out: Male Cell, MACDONALD, SAUNDERS.

◆ ◆ ◆ ◆ ◆

Female Wing – Education Room

Monitor(s): Female Wing. F.P.O. on duty.

Light up: JANET and HARRY.

JANET The need of the system Harry is to tactically manage. Security first. Then accommodation. Then the needs of the inmates.

HARRY I couldn't get in last week. No explanation! Just stopped at the gate. They weren't even polite. I'd driven forty miles.

'You'll still get paid.' I said, 'And are you paid extra for being rude?'

JANET — You'll get used to it... Tell the Gov...

◆ ◆ ◆ ◆ ◆

Assistant Governor's Office

Light up: A.G.

HARRY — I want to do my job... Money doesn't come into it.

A.G. — We had a suicide! In the male prison.

HARRY — Oh!

A.G. — Not the first this year...

HARRY — I didn't know.

A.G. — Association... Classes were ruled out.

HARRY — I see... Couldn't they just have told me. Why all the cloak, and dagger?

A.G. — We sit on a powder keg. A spark is all it needs... That's why I placed so much store on someone like you coming in. Something for them to look forward to. Contact with the outside world... Something to restore part of their humanity... I don't want that frustrated... The Prison Officers Association Harry... No! I won't say it... All I ask of you, is don't deliberately run your head into a brick wall.

Fade out: A.G.'s Office.

◆ ◆ ◆ ◆ ◆

Female Wing – Education Room

Monitor(s): MARTY and BRIDGET alone in their cells. They rock silently.

JANET — There's a debate here then? Humane, and liberal A.G. is thinking aloud.

HARRY — Not fair Janet! Some of the younger ones seem very professional… dedicated!

JANET — Oh sure! Some very nice prison officers. I mean it! Really are! Yeah! But they got to have two faces. One for in here, one for when they go home.

Listen, there's a Judas hole they spy through. The boy who hanged himself smeared it with toothpaste. His cellmate laid back, let him get on with it. The men shout over. We get to know!

HARRY — You say it so casually.

JANET — I'm saying it's tough… and it's out of sight, and out of mind…

We have a girl here, wanting to go back to Holloway… Her friends can't afford to visit her. They'd return her if something was seriously, medically wrong. 'Cos they haven't a woman's hospital here. What she had in mind was a broken leg. So we broke it for her…

HARRY — You did what?

JANET — Yeah! Held her down, and smashed her shin with a flat iron. Took her to the shower, and said she'd slipped…

HARRY — How could you?

JANET Yeh! Took a bit of doin'. Had to bang it six or seven times before it cracked.

HARRY Mad!

JANET Shocked are you?

HARRY Could've crippled her for life.

JANET What do you understand? You come here for a couple of hours. You see us on association. You don't see us locked up. The rabbit hutches, twelve foot by eight. A chair, a bed, a chamber pot. Year in, year out. You don't see the head bangers. The strips… the meat safe… they go mad in there. The same bloody stone wall, the yard, no grass, no trees, no children's voices… Being grateful for an occasional kind word. You don't have to lie awake night after night, listening to someone sobbing in the next cell… No! A prisoner asks for help, you do it, no matter what… What's the good of tryin' to tell you. Here I've written you somethin'! [*Reads*] 'Me dad kept pigeons. When I was seven, one came home hurt, and he said it should be put out of it's misery. He couldn't do it 'cos it was one of his favourites. Me brother wouldn't do it either, but I did it… Me dad give us a beltin' but he was cryin'… I buried it in a place of grass, and nettles, but wild cats came, and took it away.'

I've stood on a chair and seen a sunset over the cathedral and wept feeling jealous of all things free…

HARRY Inside, it's just as dark, and uncomfortable as any other pile of stone.

JANET Yeh!

HARRY Sunlight and air! People need that more than anything.

JANET So what's missing?

HARRY The recuperative power of nature.

JANET What would you do with us Harry?

HARRY Get a bus and take you all up to the Cheviot Hills.

Fade out: Female Wing – Education Room.

◆ ◆ ◆ ◆ ◆

Male Wing – Education Room

Monitor(s): M.P.O.s with dogs. Male prisoners shuffle round exercise yard.

Light up: ACKROYD.

ACKROYD There y'are sir [*Hands HARRY two exercise books*]

HARRY Harry!

ACKROYD There y'are Harry sir!

HARRY What's this?

ACKROYD Me story.

HARRY All this?

ACKROYD No good is it?

HARRY Hold on! Let me look!

ACKROYD Don't let them see. I'm not crawlin'.

HARRY [*Reads*] 'Into care… ten and a half!'

ACKROYD Twelve when a went to Approved School!

HARRY [*Reads*] '"Its for your own good Billy", the magistrate said.'

ACKROYD Was a friggin' nightmare. Axwell Park. Aycliffe. Was lads there fifteen, sixteen. Y'know, used ti climb in yor bed. Nowt the little'uns could do . Cry for thor mams.

HARRY This your record?

ACKROYD Yeh!

HARRY You are thirty five? Thirty seven?

ACKROYD Yeh!

HARRY Spent fifteen years inside?

ACKROYD Yeh!

HARRY 'Coming Home.' Read this to me.

ACKROYD What? Out loud.

HARRY Yes.

ACKROYD Nah! You read it!

HARRY [*Reads*] 'Easter came round. How happy that made me! Mr Jones got us up at four in the morning. Sixty of us, in our new clothes with white armbands. We marched in twos down to the bus-stop at Egremont… When we got in sight of Blaydon…'

ACKROYD A could see the chimney pots. Home! An' no polis lookin' for me, even if it was only for a week.

HARRY [*Reads*] 'You never forget the feeling inside of the sight of the place where you belong…'

ACKROYD Newcastle was my home!

HARRY [*Reads*] 'I had a feeling of belonging…'

ACKROYD Like that song… *This is my Country*. Man! The joy of pullin' into the terminus at the bottom of Fawdon Road. A wanted to run and scream.

HARRY [*Reads*] 'This feeling of love was beyond belief. All smartly dressed with me Italian suit, bag in hand, me head was up. I hadn't seen me parents for a long time. I walked unsteadily at first, afraid, looking around. Halfway to the flats I saw my brother George… I shouted his name.'

ACKROYD 'George! George!' He looked an' put his head down. He was talkin' to a smaller lad, and took no notice of me… I shouted again…'George!' He stared. An' all of a sudden he ran to me… 'Its our Billy… our Billy!' He flew into me arms. He was only six or seven. The lad that was with him was about five but I didn't know who he was. He moved up closely and put a hand across me coat bottom. George said 'It's our Chris, Billy!' I put George down an' picked up

Chris. A was tongue tied. A cuddled him. 'You're a big lad.'

HARRY [*Reads*] 'And off we went, me carrying Chris and George running ahead to tell our folks. Before I got to the flat I seen me mam and sisters at the window. I waved and they waved then I went into the block. First thing I noticed the coal sheds… Bad memories there, and a went upstairs.'

ACKROYD Me mother had the door open. I stood! Our Florence was there, Elizabeth! Me two oldest sisters. Then a seen a shy quiet girl. Me youngest sister Margaret. She'd grown long, lovely black hair, an' there was our Stan… 'Hi Billy.' 'Hi Stan.' It was so strange. I was a stranger. Me family were strange. But there was love for each other, an the smiles were long… Me dad broke the ice… Let'im in! C'mon let'im in!

[*HARRY embraces ACKROYD. M.P.O. enters leading ACKROYD off*]

Fade out: Male Wing – Education Room.

◆ ◆ ◆ ◆ ◆

Assistant Governor's Office

Monitor(s): Empty corridors.

Light up: A.G.

A.G. Success then!

HARRY All I'd asked.

A.G. Good!

HARRY So fluid, you wanted it to go on... a revelation! What has happened to them George? Yesterday they were children.

M.P.O. (O.S.) Are the Cac's on?

M.P.O. 2 (O.S.) [*Answers*] Cac's on!

A.G. Centralised Automatic Control System! Computer speak for 'banging up'...

M.P.O. [*Returns*] Ready for rounds, sir.

A.G. Is it not a widely held public view that unless the criminal suffers, the crime is somehow condoned?

HARRY You don't believe that?

A.G. The Judain/Christian concept Harry. Reward for doing good has no merit, unless by the same token, wrongdoers get their comeuppance.

HARRY [*To audience*] First thing I noticed... the smell! If I had to give it a name I'd say despairing.

A.G. Goodnight Harry!

M.P.O. Goodnight sir!

[*A.G. and M.P.O. exit*]

HARRY Goodnight George! We'll take it up again next time.

[*To the audience*] But above me hope gathered on the lintels, like the gossip of the starlings.

Fade out: A.G.'s Office

MALE 1 (O.S.) [*Whistles*] Y'there Stew?

MALE 2 (O.S.) Alright Alfie?

MALE 1 (O.S.) Watcha doin?

MALE 2 (O.S.) Havin' a crap.

MALE 1 (O.S.) Hurry up! Lights out!

MALE 3 (O.S.) What yer in for?

MALE 4 (O.S.) Burglary.

MALE 3 (O.S.) Got yer P.E.D. yet?

MALE 4 (O.S.) Two year.

MALE 3 (O.S.) Bed and Breakfast man.

MALE 1 (O.S.) Hey Bridget! How's yer tits?

FEMALE Push off.

MALE 1 (O.S.) Wish a could.

MALE 2 (O.S.) Where e from Bridget?

FEMALE County Galway!

MALE 2 (O.S.) I'm from Mars…

FEMALE You sound spaced out…

MALE 1 (O.S.) Us Geordie boys don't piss about. We do wor bird an' get straightened out.

MALE 2 (O.S.) Where's Macsi?

MALE 3 (O.S.) In the cage.

MALE 2 (O.S.) How's your lass Alfie?

MALE 1 (O.S.) She put a disc on Metro for us.

MALE 2 (O.S.) What was it?

MALE 1 (O.S.) 'I have sinned'!

MALE 2 (O.S.) Friggin hell!

[*HARRY walks off. Exits. Light off*]

MALE 1 (O.S.) She wants us to get married… A don't know what to do Stew. She's got four kids…

FEMALE What would she want to marry you for?

MALE 1 (O.S.) Dunno! Me mam says A'm daft…

FEMALE Yer mam's right…

MALE 2 (O.S.) What d'ye think she's after, Alfie?

MALE 1 (O.S.) Dunno! A think she's lookin for security!

END OF FIRST ACT

Act Two

The Apron Stage

Monitor(s): The prison gates.

Light up: HARRY.

HARRY — [*To the audience*] Inside! You meet all kinds. Like the Bishop of Durham. I was introduced.

'Do you think', I said, 'they steer you round, making sure you only see what they want you to see?'

Cups a quizzical hand to his ear. As though he was hard of hearing, or maybe I was not speaking clearly.

'Yes! Yes! I think so, but there are other ways of gaining a true impression.'

Later, in the company of the Governor, we were walking through the compound when we were ambushed...

VOICE FROM ABOVE — All screws are bastards!

HARRY — [*Cupping his ear*] I don't think he can be that hard of hearing... Anyway, I got the point...

◆ ◆ ◆ ◆ ◆

Female Wing – Education Room

Monitor(s): F.P.O. unlocking a gate. HARRY comes into view and passes through. F.P.O. closes the gate, occupies the screen, full face. SANDRA comes behind the F.P.O. then passes through.

Light up: JANET writing, SANDRA reading a letter. Enter HARRY. Places his tape recorder on the ironing board.

SANDRA Janet… spare us a word…

JANET For you Sandra… a word…

SANDRA Sorry to interrupt mister.

HARRY It's alright…

SANDRA It's the Noddy Shop Janet. A've gotta get out. It's killin' us… the boredom!

JANET What ye's makin'?

SANDRA Sodden teddy bears, an' draft excluders.

JANET Be subtle Sandra… convince them ye'll cut up…

SANDRA But the' trust me wi' scissors…

JANET Can't understand why…

SANDRA Neither do I…

JANET Mess the job up…

SANDRA What can ye do ti draft excluders?

JANET Not them! The teddy bears? That's it… every third teddy… put it's feet on back ti front.

SANDRA	Ye think that'll work?
JANET	Gotta convince the A.G. yor neurotic.
SANDRA	But I am neurotic…
JANET	I know yor neurotic Sandra. We all know that… but the A.G. needs evidence.
HARRY	Couldn't you write a petition?
SANDRA	I don't read or write mister. I used ti get letters. Didn't I Janet? I used ti get a lot o' letters. But the' stopped sendin' them 'cos I didn't reply…
JANET	Don't upset yorself…
SANDRA	Classes is it ye do here?
HARRY	Would you like to…
SANDRA	I always wanted ti be a plumber. Is that right mister, the men get on courses like brick layin', an' plumbin'?
HARRY	I've heard that…
JANET	Sandra! Ye drowned yor old man in the bath, wouldn't plumbin' bring it all back?
SANDRA	[*SANDRA pauses to think*] Yor right! A wouldn't want that bugga back.

Fade out: Female Wing – Education Room.

◆ ◆ ◆ ◆ ◆

Female Cell

Monitor(s): The cell block.

Light up: BRIDGET and HARRY.

BRIDGET Harry man! A cannit get this right.

HARRY Let's see!

BRIDGET [*With letter*] Dear Mrs Holder. I am writin' ti you, as I wish to see Elaine, an' Sean… It's destroyin' me each day, thinkin' what is happenin' ti my babies. How do you know how they will react to seein' me in here… [*Hands the letter over to HARRY*]

HARRY [*Reads*] 'I do not think you or anyone in the department realises what you do to a person… I love my children regardless of what I have done.'

That sounds alright Bridget… it's fine.

BRIDGET No! looka the spellin'…

HARRY Say what you have to say Bridget, and write the way you talk… [*Switches on his tape*] C'mon…

BRIDGET It's like a vicious circle… Y'see I was put into care when I was three, an' a half, but I always wondered where my muther an' father was, an' why the' wasn't lookin' for me… When I got ti sixteen, I'd give up hope of ever knowin' who the' were… When this happened!

I was workin' in a hostel run by nuns in Glasgow. Y'know, where owld people an' travellers come in for a rest, an' a cup o' tea. I got on talkin' wi' this owld lady about where she come from, an' told her about the troubles I'd been in.

'Donachie!' she said, 'Is that your name?' 'Would ye know an Annie Donachie?'

An' I remembered I'd had a sister of that name.

'Well love, I'm yor grandmother…'

She directed me to me family who were livin' on a site near Manchester, an' that's the livin' truth how I got back to them.

But I never forgive me muther for not fightin' for me. When she died I was the only one who didn't cry at the funeral.

She said, because of what she'd done, they'd declared her not to be a fit parent. But I felt, if she'd really loved me, she would have fought for me.

Now I'm in the same trouble. My two youngest are fostered while I'm in here, and they never write. I don't know if they are gettin' me letters, and I don't even know the name, and address of where they are fostered. Mrs Holder won't tell me. She says she can't! Can you tell me what I should do Harry? I don't want me kids growin' up thinkin' about me, the way I thought about me muther.

◆ ◆ ◆ ◆ ◆

Assistant Governor's Office

Monitor(s): M.P.O. with dog, patrols.

Light up: A.G.

HARRY — She thought I'd written it… I had to play it back to convince her. George man! Progress! But twelve weeks! Its not long enough. What I wanted to ask. I'd come for nothing. If you could arrange an extension. I'd keep it up, and it wouldn't cost the department a penny…

A.G. — I'll put it to the governor. I must tell you that we are a little concerned. Personally, I think you could be doing a good job… There are some bizarre people Harry! We worry all the time. Some you wouldn't dare let out… What do you do with the monsters?

◆ ◆ ◆ ◆ ◆

Female Wing – Education Room

Monitor(s): Two F.P.O.'s in corridor.

Light up: SHARON, JANET and HARRY.

SHARON — Sharon Jackson! 33225.

Join the friggin' queue.

I'm not sayin' which prison this was Harry, 'cos you could get me on report… But *SHE* was there! They give me the *News of The World*. There's this disgustin' article about *HER*. I couldn't bear it. The Governor said it was to be banned off the wing, but they give it me.

Monitor(s): Two F.P.O.s glance out of the screen.

Made me sick, what she did to those kids, and I mean, I wasn't even born when she done that crime.

[*Light up: A woman dries her hair*]

They kept out the way, an' she come to the recess. [*SHARON moves to the woman*] I knew what I had to do. [*Seizing the woman by the hair. She punches her repeatedly*] You bastard! You bastard! [*Swings the woman round. An unrecognisable, bloody mask of face. She allows the woman to fall. Fade out woman*] I didn't go on report. 'Sit down Sharon.' 'Take it easy…' 'Calm yourself.' 'We've wanted ti do that for a long time.'

They give me a cup o' tea, an' some sweets. But I wish now… I hadn't let meself get so wound up.

JANET Yeh! She was here. Remember me mam on her first visit. She'd never been in prison before.

MAM [*Light up*] Alright luv?

JANET Alright mam?

MAM What's the grub like?

JANET Alright mam.

MAM Lookin' a bit thin.

JANET Yes mam.

MAM I don't like these places Janet.

JANET That's two of us mam.

MAM Jan?

JANET Yes mam.

MAM Is *SHE* here?

JANET Y'what?

MAM Y'know… *HER*… is she here?

JANET What y'talkin' about mam?

MAM *HER*! Y'know.

JANET Who di ye mean? Who y'ron about?

MAM Ssssh! Y'know… *HER*.

JANET Oh' … I said. Y'mean Myra!… Hey' Myra this is me mam.

MAM 'Cos she was in the visitin' on the other side of the room.

JANET Me mam near passed out…

MAM Janet! Ye shouldn't talk ti people like that. [*Fade out*]

Monitor(s): Corridor. Barred window.

HARRY But you do?

JANET We had two goody-goodies here. Ten years an' they never went on report. Always readin' the lives o' the saints! But they wouldn't go to mass if she was there… kind o' faith is that? Dear Jesus, we love you, but we'll have us own rules.

Like Magilligan. The UDA won't mix with the IRA, an' likewise. Friggin' crazy. It's in here we come together, or nowhere! In here we can look inside ourselves, see what we really are. If there's hope at all, it begins here… 'cos it's the bottom of the world. You wanna save yorself from monsters, you gotta talk to them.

[*Enter MARTY*]

JANET — We're talkin' about killin' people Marty. Like murder! Go on tell us… Are you gonna say somethin'… Go on Marty… What's it all about? Tell us about yor stabbin'… Tell us about the geezer you brown breaded. Was you in a temper? Did he provoke you?

[*MARTY sits on the floor. Head between her knees. Rocking back and forward*]

Come on! Sufferin' from P.M.T. at the time was you? Was 'e touchin' ye up or somethin'? You told me! Go on you can tell Harry. You can tell his little machine. 'Cos of men, an, yor body, an' the way they used you wasn't it? Well go on Marty! Do you feel guilty? Do you get dreams?

Monitor(s) F.P.O. comes full face on the screen.

She feels extremely guilty Harry, and extremely sorry, but she don't want to admit it. It's not done in prison.

MARTY — No… no!

JANET — Go on then for fuck's sake, contradict me!

MARTY — Piss off!

JANET [*JANET goes to MARTY and hugs her. MARTY returns the embrace. They rock gently together*] There. S'alright Marty… S'alright! Ssssh! S'alright!

HARRY Are you a monster Janet?

JANET Course I am. Looka me two heads. Looka me horns.

HARRY Do you believe in killing?

JANET Says so in the book don't it.

HARRY No! The record says, 'It is not the case for the crown that you placed the bomb, but that you liaised with those persons unknown who did…'

JANET Oh! Been readin' transcripts have we?

HARRY Yes!

JANET Pluckin' up courage to ask the big question.

HARRY Yes!

JANET Signed a confession… didn't I.

HARRY Who doesn't these days? They dismissed it. Threw it out. A bomb goes off in a public place. An hour later you appear, drunk, and disorderly shouting 'Up the IRA.'

JANET Yeh… good old Gerry Adams…

HARRY Would a member of an Active Service Unit do that?

Monitor(s): External walls.

JANET — What would you know what we have to do? You know nothing…

HARRY — I know… the death of children solves nothing…

JANET — Oh 'friggin brilliant that… You tell'm that in Chatila! Tell'm that in Divis… You ever been to Beirut Harry? Ever been to Belfast? Then what would you know?

Fade out: Female Wing – Education Room.

◆ ◆ ◆ ◆ ◆

Assistant Governor's Office

A.G. — [*Light up*] What the hell do you think you are doing? We've people for that sort of thing. Chaplains, psychologists. For God's sake, you listen to them they're all innocent.

HARRY — But there are some… It's becoming clear… The Guildford four… the Birmingham five.

A.G. — I am a prison administrator, my job…

HARRY — What if you became convinced of someone's innocence?

A.G. — Remain a prison administrator… Not you Harry… you are not qualified. It is not why you are here… Leave it!

[*Enter M.P.O.*]

A.G. Ah! James Albert Laidler! Now this is the character! The oldest recidivist in the prison. You must meet him Harry. [*Hands HARRY a record card*]

[*To the M.P.O.*] Do the honours will you.

M.P.O. Sir!

Fade out: A.G.'s Office.

◆ ◆ ◆ ◆ ◆

Male Cell

Monitor(s): Cell door.

Light up: A man lies in his bunk. Only his head is visible. His hair is white.

M.P.O. Albert! Wakey! Wakey! You've got a visitor…

HARRY He's asleep… leave'm.

M.P.O. No! Likes to chat does Albert! C'mon Albert. Someone to see you.

ALBERT [*ALBERT raises himself on one elbow*] Who are y?

HARRY Hello Albert. You got a story for me?

ALBERT Eh?

HARRY Just putting the machine on…

ALBERT What's he sayin'?

[*The M.P.O. exits. Stands to one side*]

HARRY — [*Into his tape-recorder*] James Albert Laidler… born 1917 in Gateshead County Durham… At this moment in a cell eight foot by twelve. Time of recording November 1986.

ALBERT — What's that?

HARRY — How do you keep warm Albert?

ALBERT — Keep under a blanket…

HARRY — His skin like wax, ears and eyelids pink, translucent. Hair… white!

Monitor(s): Cell door.

ALBERT — When A was five. A was sent ti the Abbot Memorial Industrial School. The masters was very strict.

HARRY — Where on Christmas day, the mayor and councillors of Gateshead served Christmas pudding to the cheers of ragged lads.

ALBERT — At nine, transferred us ti Axwell Park Approved School. A stayed there 'till A was sixteen.

HARRY — And learned reading and writing. Took to the heart the Catechism, and was confirmed by the Bishop of Jarrow.

ALBERT — But man, a couldn't curb mesel'… Runnin' away! Ti fairgrounds an' roundabouts! Always got caught… The thought A was mental, y'knaa. Sent us ti Shotley Bridge Mental Colony.

HARRY — What about your father and mother Albert?

ALBERT — Me mother come… Me father never did. A cannit remember now! Was A thirteen or fourteen when me mother stopped comin'? A kept watch out the winder every week-end but she stopped comin'.

HARRY — The Prudhoe Hall.

ALBERT — Run away fifty three times from there. A once run away in me night shirt. All the way over the fields ti Sunderland.

Durin the war wi got vouchers, but A gave me chocolate ti Mr. Fothergill for his two children, 'cos he was good ti me.

HARRY — A stolen suitcase… King's Cross Station. Nine months… Wormwood Scrubs.

ALBERT — Doctors were very good there. Give us A certificate sayin' a was of sound mind.

HARRY — Transfer to Feltham Borstal… stolen suitcase, Newcastle Central Station… two years, Durham.

Two cushion covers, two pillow cases from Bainbridges three years hard labour.

Another suitcase… another three and a half years…

Two shirts from the Salvation Army. Seven years… preventive detention…

Four bottles of sweets… six years…

Albert! You have spent forty of your sixty years in prison…

Why?

ALBERT	Divvent knaa! Y'see when A was four me father give us a beltin' for runnin' off. So a stole some sweets... Look. A've gorra florin. Y'know the old two bob? Can y'see the dates on it? Turn it upside down. Y'see the I.L.L.I. of shillin is 1771.
HARRY	Very good.
ALBERT	Can y'see the pub?
HARRY	No.
ALBERT	There! The Queen's Head!
HARRY	Albert!
ALBERT	Just a minute. What about the three Irishmen?
HARRY	Where are they Albert?
ALBERT	In the Queen's head. A'm not daft y'knaaa!
HARRY	Of course you aren't!
ALBERT	Y'comin' ti see us again mister?
HARRY	I hope so...
ALBERT	Me father y'see. He was a polis! A think he felt ashamed of us...

Fade out: Male Cell.

◆ ◆ ◆ ◆ ◆

Assistant Governor's Office

Monitor(s): M.P.O. with dog. Prisoners exercise.

Light up: A.G.

A.G. The good news and the good news! Which do you want first?

HARRY Ackroyd has been paroled!

A.G. That's right! Left you a letter. I think he'd like to keep in touch... You must have struck a chord. Never give them your address. You realise that?

HARRY It's pathetic!... And?

A.G. And... you can continue in the women's wing until further notice... from the Governor...

HARRY Oh!

A.G. Cheer up!

HARRY Yes

A.G. We aren't pretending prison is reformative Harry. Ten years ago... twenty five thousand. Today fifty thousand. It's beyond us.

Fade out: A.G.'s Office.

HARRY [*To the audience*] Old Albert you see. He'd got to me! What's the point? Do we really need a fortress to contain the shell of a man?

◆ ◆ ◆ ◆ ◆

Prison Yard

Monitor(s): Blank

Light up: M.P.O.

M.P.O. You have permission for that recorder?

HARRY Not again! Yes, I have permission from the Governor.

M.P.O. You may have the Governor's permission, but you haven't got mine... If my voice goes on there I'll sue you.

HARRY Will you?

M.P.O. Oh yes!

HARRY Why?

M.P.O. I just don't want my voice on there...

HARRY It's not likely...

M.P.O. Just remember...

HARRY Is that what you have to say?

M.P.O. Come here sympathising with them. Gettin' their stories! What about our stories?

HARRY Would you like to tell me one?

M.P.O. Bloody sure I wouldn't. No way.

HARRY Then you'll have nothing to complain about...

M.P.O. — I just don't trust people like you.

Fade out: Prison Yard.

◆ ◆ ◆ ◆ ◆

Assistant Governor's Office

Monitor(s): Prison corridor.

Light up: A.G.

A.G. — A persistent thief Harry.

HARRY — But the punitive nature of it. Poor old sod. Other than a miserable neglected life... what's his share been?

A.G. — Suitcases!

HARRY — Snatching a few baubles from the travelling public.

A.G. — Would you like it if they were yours?

HARRY — The little comfort of a jar of toffees. Could've put his life's crime on a kitchen table... Does it redress the balance. A broken old man in a box.

A.G. — But who's arguing?

HARRY — Insider dealers make millions... impoverish thousands. They don't suffer the same fate.

A.G. — Your mistake Harry… is equating the prison service with judicial unfairness. You are making the prison staff the focal point of your view of social injustice… Now that is not on! It is not fair! We are minding the mess. Give us a break.

Fade out: A.G.'s Office.

◆ ◆ ◆ ◆ ◆

Female Wing – Education Room

Monitor(s): Two F.P.O.s relax on the landing.

Light up: JANET.

JANET — He's right. But it's what they all want. People get satisfaction believing the wicked are sufferin'. Don't matter who's in here, so long as someone is. Revenge is very popular Harry. I'm not incapable of the feeling. You should come to terms with it.

HARRY — There is a state of mind Janet that takes no account of revenge, and it is just as fulfilling. Have you written something for me?

JANET — You a Quaker Harry?

HARRY — Why do you always answer a question with a question?

JANET — Who? Me? Harry, I've been grilled by the Army, the R.U.C., the Special Branch… I'm an expert at counter interrogation.

HARRY You didn't save yourself at your trial...

JANET No!

HARRY Could you have?

JANET Why do you ask?

HARRY Could you?

JANET By putting six others where I am. I'd never do that... would I?

Fade out: Female Wing – Education Room.

◆ ◆ ◆ ◆ ◆

Exit on the Female Wing

Monitor(s): F.P.O. walks through the screen.

Light up: F.P.O.

INTERCOM [*Buzzes*]

F.P.O. Control!

INTERCOM Control!

F.P.O. Education staff ready to leave the wing.

INTERCOM Two minutes!

F.P.O. Right! [*To HARRY*] Won't be long sir.

HARRY Thank you...

F.P.O. May I see inside your case sir.

HARRY Of course…

F.P.O. You've permission for this haven't you?

HARRY Yes.

F.P.O. Thank you…

HARRY Time will you finish?

F.P.O. 9 p.m.

HARRY Long day!

F.P.O. Need the overtime.

You know… when I first came here… I'd read the newspaper headlines… and I thought… you know… My God! I was prepared to hate them! Meeting them was a surprise, they bore no resemblance to what I'd read.

You don't realise you can be so manipulated. Your conscience, your judgement… it's only what you are told… or not told. I mean, it just isn't safe is it, making your mind up on scraps of information. I had to come here to find that out. [*Hands back the case. Loud clicking sound*] That's the electronic lock off sir… The gate is open. Thank you! Have a safe journey.

Fade out: Female Wing.

◆ ◆ ◆ ◆ ◆

Male Cell

Monitor(s): Cell door.

Light up: PRISONER 7527, with back to the audience.

HARRY — [*Into his tape-recorder*] 7527. 'C' Wing. November 3rd. Name withheld. Prison Act 1952.

[*Light up: MACDONALD. Dressed in one piece smock. Fastened at wrists and ankles. He lies on a mat groaning*]

Monitor(s): Shows film.[1]

7527 — The Meat Safe! I'm sorry if he's in there! Christ! Nine days!

MACDONALD — Please! Please!

7527 — I mean he's a bastard! I've said to him 'You think you're famous Macsi. Nobody's famous here.'

HARRY — Why?

7527 — Use it against me.

HARRY — You've come on education…

7527 — When A get out. A want to write.

MACDONALD — Oh for Chris' sake. Please! Please! Somebody! Somebody!

---

[1] *Look North* Film of Frankland Segregation Cell. Shown 23. 5. 1987.

7527 — Y'lose all sense of time. Y'get desperate. A've seen really big men come out cryin'.

HARRY — What's your story?

7527 — A stabbed our lass! It was terrible! We'd just gorra house. A was in work. A was a plasterer. Good money! Don' know what happened really. A'm a bit jealous like!

An a don' wanna make excuses ! A've never been in trouble before. This is me first time inside… A loved her. Just couldn't control what was happenin' She's forgiven us like! Don' know why. A'm hangin' on ti that. A've got four years.

MACDONALD — Muther! Muther!

7527 — A was on remand. She was in hospital. A didn't know if she was gonna live. The' wouldn't tell us. Couldn't get ti know… Really loved her y'know! A was upset.

HARRY — Couldn't get to know?

7527 — Aye! Any news! Was she alive or dead.

MACDONALD — Oh Jesus! Please somebody. Please come! Somebody!

7527 — A was gettin' these headaches. Terrible pains… about here [*touches his temple*]. Went on for three days. So I asked for the M.O.L. He was called Battery Charger! Like a mock of his name that was… I know now. He had a reputation. A think they've shifted him.

'Have you a depression?'

'A've got these pains sir.'

'Is it a depression you've got?'

'it's in the front of me head sir.'

'Is it a depression?'

'Well if you think that's what it is, sir!'

'Officer! Depression!'

[*MACDONALD sits up. Rocks. Moans*]

7527 This screw stood me in front of a door.

'Take yer clothes off'.

Ye don't argue. When A was naked he opened the door. There was another door to the right.

'Put this on.'

Was like a hard smock... Opened the second door... A was like in a little room wit no windows. Above me a kind of funnel to a light where the' could watch ye from... No bed! A mat on the floor! Y'eat your food off the floor, like a dog. A was just in three days... Y'see nobody... Man! A wouldn't report it. A think the' give ye a chair now, but it's made out o' cardboard... 'Cos men go mad in there. Poor Macsi.

Fade out: MACDONALD and 7527.

◆◆◆◆◆

Assistant Governor's Office

Monitor(s): Prison exterior.

Light up: A.G.

A.G.	You don't have to tell me Harry! I saw the *Look North* programme. As far as silent cells go they are kept in as the officer explained, for as long as necessary. The rules require no more than twenty days at a stretch.
HARRY	But they repeat the periods…
A.G.	Surprised they got permission to film. Power of the BBC eh! But you must admit they were very open about it… No! I don't doubt your man's word. I wouldn't dream of asking you to betray a confidence… But they will play on your sympathies…
HARRY	About judicial unfairness, you made the point.
A.G.	What point?
HARRY	About the focus… Well I'm making the point. All this retribution is what is available to the courts…

Fade out: A.G.'s Office.

◆ ◆ ◆ ◆ ◆

Female Wing – Education Room

Monitor(s): F.P.O.'s in corridor.

Light up: JANET.

JANET	Where were we Harry?
HARRY	I don't like pain.
JANET	You don't like pain?
HARRY	Not for myself or anyone…
JANET	It's essential… for survival.
HARRY	I mean causing pain for no other reason than causing pain.
JANET	Who does that?
HARRY	You tell me.
JANET	You mean mankind?
HARRY	Be specific Janet…
JANET	It's love man!
HARRY	What?
JANET	The course of all this madness…
PAT	[*Enters*] 'Ere I written you somefink.
HARRY	Good… you are…?
PAT	Pat!
HARRY	Yes… of course… Pat!

PAT I done seven year for supplyin' 'eroin. Yeh! Well I fort there was nuffink morally wrong. To be honest I still fink that, but I ain't puttin' that in writin! 'Ere you are! It was 'cos of people like you… [*Reads*] I was in love wiv Miss Turnbull, me English literature teacher, I started usin' drugs when I was fifteen. Miss Turnbull told me all abaht the English romantic poets bein' into laudanum, an' opium, an' that. Coleridge, Browning, Thomas De Quincey an' that! An' don' forget old Q.V. used to 'ave it for 'er 'eadaches… but that didn't influence me…

JANET What the hell you on about Pat?

PAT I wanted to write poetry. That's why I became an addict.

JANET You mean a freakin' junkie.

PAT Not at all! There's a subtle diff'rence.

JANET Yeah! What's that?

PAT You gotta picture in yor 'ead, of all these bar freaks, an' mules up the 'dilly.

JANET Hold on! Hold on! We're leavin' Harry out…

PAT Sorry 'arry…

JANET What my cell sister is saying… Up the 'dilly… Piccadilly! Bar freaks… barbiturate users! Mules!

PAT 'Em as does the 'umpy… Tests the water! 'En's up in a jam roll…

[*Pause*]

HARRY I see!

JANET There are girls in here Harry, who never touch the stuff, but they pushed it, an' they don't give a damn if it was ten year old kids…

PAT That is wrong that is. You are outa order.

JANET Do us a favour Pat…

PAT Wassat?

JANET Piss off!

PAT Naw listen!

JANET Should lock you sods up, an' throw away the key…

PAT Yeh! I'm guilty! Proven! No argy! But there's Paki guys up in Sheffy got two 'ouses… Mercs… the lot! I could take you… right! They never touch the stuff. They's got farms in Pakistan. Big killin'! Cut the stuff wiv terrible things. Talcum powder is one of 'em. Paricetymol! Morgadon is common practice.

BRIDGET [*Enters*] Harry, you listen to them, they tell you anythin'… I can tell you…

HARRY What is it Bridget…

BRIDGET She told us. She done it alright. She ain't sorry. Them kids… She should talk… Nobody's got the right to kill kids… Two faced she is… Don' trust nothin' she tells you.

GINGER [*Enters*] 'Scuse me… are you the man?

JANET Christ! Another one… What they doin' puttin' nuttas like you in with me.

PAT Yeah! What you wantin' Ginger?

GINGER Is this the writin' class?

JANET Naw! It's the loony bin.

GINGER Here, you! Mister! Read this…

We was arrested for murder. We hadn't done no murder. Just my friends mother died. She was eighty… what they expect? Was only 'cos we buried her without tellin' nobody…

It's all in here… Read it… [*Hands over an exercise book*]

HARRY Right!… er… thanks!

PAT What concentrates yor thoughts then?

JANET Escape!

PAT Yeah! Well 'ave a fink abaht the laundry basket…

JANET Y'reckon!

PAT Yeah! Jus' 'ave a fink…

GINGER We illegally buried her like. I gotta admit that. No coroner or nothin'… Trouble was, it was like two year before the police come… An' when they says, 'Where you put her then?' Honest to God we couldn't bloody remember.

PAT — 'Sall in 'ere 'arry. Like this friend of mine is arguin', nuffink morally wrong wiv drugs.

I said, 'But Ramsey dear, there's a lotta bad Karma attached to it.'

'Ow can that be my dear?'

'Don' be so stupid Ramsey' I said, 'All these people comin' rahnd for gear! Where they getting' the readies?'

'Burglary, an' cheques,' 'e says!

I says, 'There's yer bad Karma then.'

GINGER — An' the judge says ti me 'Why did you steal five chickens?'

I says, 'It were Christmas yor honour, an' nothin', in the house…'

He says, 'You, your husband, and two children are four persons, but you stole five chickens… you are a greedy woman.'

S'all in there! All what I had to put up with…

[*Enters JORDAN*].

HARRY — Mrs Jordan! How are you? Come in…

JORDAN — Very well thank you…

HARRY — Well, good to see you again. Well, under the circumstances…

[*GINGER stamps on the floor*]

PAT — 'Ere what you do that for?

BRIDGET — Wassup?

PAT — Ginger! She stood on a bleedin' cockroach…

GINGER — Didn't stand on it…

PAT — Yes you freakin' did. You go an' get the eggs all over yor shoes… silly cow…

BRIDGET — Yeh!… Silly cow!

PAT — Spread 'em all over… Gawd!

JORDAN — This is where I came you see… I was awarded seven years…

HARRY — Awarded?

JORDAN — Not too bad eh? Oh all the lies came out. Well, we expected that. Children are very well. Love their gran. She's been super.

HARRY — The hotel? The yacht in Marbella?

JORDAN — All behind us. All forgotten. And I've made a wonderful discovery. I'm going to survive all this… For the first time in my life. I feel I am with real people.

Fade out: Female Wing – Education Room.

◆ ◆ ◆ ◆ ◆

Assistant Governor's Office

Monitor(s): Prison exterior.

Light up: HARRY takes a seat. A.G. furtively scans the corridor, closes the door, blanks the monitors.

A.G. [*Returning to pour coffee*] There you are… [*Hands cup over*]

HARRY Thanks. Does it breed contempt George…?

A.G. I've seen staff come here like knights in shining armour.

HARRY If it's all to be explained as inadequacy, or plain bloody wickedness…

A.G. End up doing other people's dirty work… I could've been a solicitor.

HARRY Are we on course again for another *final solution*?

A.G. We released a rapist after seven years. Committed the same offence within twenty four hours… I'd like that explained…

HARRY But you must know George… In the short time I've been here. This with my own eyes… On the male wing. A cell wall covered with obscene pictures of women… He was rule 43. A nonce! George! He'd been convicted of incest…

A.G. Well I deplore it…

HARRY He was sitting drawing a crucifix.

A.G. The rule is, if a magazine is lawfully on sale outside, it can lawfully be brought in.

HARRY — But what is to countervail it? Look you have a man for seven years! Now we're talking about monsters.

A.G. — Sometimes I enjoy these chats with you Harry.

HARRY — What about the monsters outside? Dirty book publishers? Porno video makers? Finding a market in the unprepared, inadequate mind?

A.G. — There is a struggle going on… A crazy young gunman slaughters his neighbours, and the President of the U.S.A. says, '*Rambo*! That's my kinda film.' We just pick up the debris…

A.G. — [*Phone rings*] Hello! A.G.

[*To HARRY*] We have to cope…

Hello! Yes! Oh God! Right! Yes, I'll be right over… [*Phone off. To HARRY*] Look! There'll be no classes tonight. This… absolutely to yourself, the Hungarian girl… Maria. Did you know her?

HARRY — I've never met her. The girls have talked about her… Murdered her young son.

A.G. — She's hanged herself…

Fade out: A.G.'s Office

◆ ◆ ◆ ◆ ◆

Female Cell

Monitor(s): Cell door.

Light up: JANET in her cell.

JANET — She was a quiet polite woman. We all liked her. It would have been her boy's birthday this Saturday. Her husband sent a little kid's birthday card. It had the son's name on it… It must have been the last straw. She'd been asking to see the shrink, but no one was taking any notice. She went to her room… they always prefer that word to cell… and she hung herself. She first of all put a cloth around her face, and plugged up all her… openings! That's how thoughtful she was… We could hear them carrying her downstairs in a box… We weren't unlocked until 11a.m. exercise… By tea-time though, everything was back to normal.

Fade out: Female Cell.

◆ ◆ ◆ ◆ ◆

Female Cell Block

Monitor(s): Cell block. F.P.O.s on duty.

Light up: MARTY accompanied by F.P.O.

HARRY — Hello Marty… how are you?

MARTY — Alright!

[*The F.P.O. stands to one side*]

HARRY You haven't been to the class…

MARTY No! I haven't been well. It's one of those things.

HARRY Shame…

F.P.O. Come along sir… these girls have a job to do…

HARRY Sorry!

MARTY [*Confidentially*] They want me to have an operation, but I'm only twenty one, an' I'm fightin' them.

HARRY Oh! You take care of yourself then.

MARTY Yeh! You see I still want to have kids.

HARRY Tomorrow you'll feel better…

F.P.O. Sir!

MARTY You know… when I went back to the flat… I took my mum. When I opened the door 'e was lyin' there in the passage in all that blood. Well I must've done it… but I wouldn' 'ave took me mum if I'd done it would I?

HARRY Marty…! [*Touches her lightly on the arm*]

[*MARTY exits*]

F.P.O. This way sir… You girls carry on!

[*Confronting HARRY*] Right! I'll give you some advice.

HARRY Yes!

F.P.O. Even the padre isn't safe in here.

HARRY You what?

F.P.O. I'm telling you… These girls never see a man from one year to the next.

HARRY Please… excuse me!

F.P.O. You listen to me.

HARRY Do you mind…

F.P.O. I am telling you… they would haul you into a cell faster than… you could imagine.

HARRY Really! Even the padre eh?

F.P.O. Yes!

HARRY Well lucky for him…

F.P.O. I am being serious…

HARRY I know you are… That's what astonishes me…

Fade out: Female Cell Block.

◆ ◆ ◆ ◆ ◆

Female Wing – Education Room

Monitor(s): F.P.O.s on duty.

Light-up.

HARRY — You remain the enigma! Queen bee of all this. Janet, I don't think I'll be around much longer…

JANET — Something you wanted to know.

HARRY — Is there any innocence here?

JANET — Is there any in the world?

HARRY — Are you?

JANET — Don't make a cause of me Harry. What would you do with my story. Hand it in to Mrs Gates?

HARRY — Not willingly.

JANET — You made'm promises. You don't have to make promises to us. What would they allow, some sanitised version? No point our writing anything real, you know that…

HARRY — Never been face to face with a famous criminal.

JANET — You can tell your friends.

HARRY — Does it involve me in some kind of responsibility?

JANET — Didn't you ask her why she done it?

HARRY — I worry about political violence. The death of innocents.

JANET Too propagandist Harry. The argument is only about the legal or the illegal use of violence. What about Dresden? What about Hiroshima?

HARRY I don't defend state violence.

JANET Are we about to argue right, and wrong, or are we going to argue about who has won an argument?

HARRY I mean, don't you think to mimic the violence of the state, you simply give each other credibility?

JANET You asking we should sit back and take it?

HARRY At least re-think your targeting.

JANET Harry! One and a quarter million Palestinian men, women and children beaten and bundled out of their homes, and sent into exile to rot and starve and die, and no one in the West gives a damn. Unless they 'explode'…

HARRY It's the same despairing game. Victory on the basis of power to dismay, and terrify the living. Bombing Hiroshima, or a pub, it's all done by very confused people.

JANET What is your alternative?

HARRY I haven't your battlefield experience.

JANET Don't patronise.

HARRY — Well, suppose you had an off duty UDR man in your sights. Instead of leaving him in a pool of blood, how about marching him off to meet your grandmother.

JANET — You what?

HARRY — Blindfolded! Take him to meet your mam, and dad, nieces, nephews. Keep him as long as necessary to learn all about your hopes, and dreams, and listen to your grandmother's stories…

JANET — You're nuts.

HARRY — No… listen! When he has taken it all to heart, and promised never to betray you, or willingly in his life to ever harm your people… you return him to his own family… without a scratch…

JANET — Harry for gawd's sake… You think he'd honour that? Besides you don't know my grandmother…

HARRY — You'd have spared his life. He'd be under a moral obligation…

JANET — You talking about magnanimity?

HARRY — That's right…

JANET — One sided magnanimity.

HARRY — One up moral superiority!

JANET — You're crazy. Those lot don't have morals.

HARRY — But they are human beings… so they can acquire them…

JANET What you asking me to believe?

HARRY That your worse enemy is a human being. Of course he might want you to meet his grandmother…

JANET You are so naive Harry! You are unbelievable. Sorry to disillusion you, but understanding only comes from the real experience of a situation.

HARRY Then you tell me what that is. What is your moral obligation. You got it locked up inside you… then bloody well unlock it. Write… for Chris' sake… write!

JANET Be a shame when they stop you comin' Harry, I really enjoy the crack.

Fade out: Female Wing – Education Room.

◆◆◆◆◆

Assistant Governor's Office

Monitor(s): Prison exterior.

Light up: HARRY and A.G.

HARRY It's just a half dozen books George. Paperbacks! I haven't sealed the Christmas wrapping… I know you'd have to examine… Maybe Christmas morning you'd do me the favour… for each of the girls.

A.G. Sure! They'll be delighted…

HARRY Thanks…

A.G.	Hazlitt! 'Hope is the best possession…'
HARRY	You familiar with Hazlitt?
A.G.	Vaguely. 'None so wretched as those without'. I've been fair with you Harry?
HARRY	Completely!
A.G.	I wanted to see a door open.
HARRY	I believe that…
A.G.	The girl you are talking to…
HARRY	Janet!
A.G.	She'd have been dead under the old rules.
HARRY	Yes!
A.G.	I am trying to be honest with you. We are not all bastards…
HARRY	Of course not.
A.G.	I know… if you deprive the human spirit of hope, you invite calamity… I know that… You can take away capital punishment, but what you cannot do is put a living being in a grave.
HARRY	George I…
A.G.	What currently is bursting out the roofs of prisons is the betrayal of hope. I know that…
HARRY	Is that room I meet the girls in bugged?

A.G. ...but the system needs to work Harry, and I know that... Finally you bring your intelligence, and wit, and a belief that you will at least be trusted... It doesn't matter... you aren't pleasing everyone... But something out of the past betrays us... Good old Gorbachev eh? He's doing it from the top... Well that's outflanking them... But they'll not forgive him... the old guard... Yes Harry, there is a struggle going on, and yes... there is a conspiracy... loosely arrived at... and you must join one camp or the other...

HARRY But they must allow hope to persist...

A.G. Absolutely! There is no other way of healing.

Fade out: A.G.'s Office.

◆ ◆ ◆ ◆ ◆

Female Wing – Education Room

Monitor(s): Corridor

Light up: JANET and HARRY.

HARRY Unless you have something to say Janet... there is no point in writing. When you were arrested you were in the middle of a city... OK it was Liverpool... right?

JANET Now what?

HARRY Is this room bugged? Do they listen?

JANET — If they do… you are gonna find out. It don't matter to me.

HARRY — Middle of Liverpool… at night… only two pound in your pocket. You couldn't afford board, and lodging… If you'd been part of that bombing operation, they wouldn't have allowed you into such a vulnerable situation. It would have endangered 'them'…

JANET — [*Yawns*] Yeah!

HARRY — You phone a friend… wait to be collected. The friend doesn't arrive but the police do…

JANET — This is all coming out of your head, not mine Harry…

HARRY — It was said in court… is it right?

JANET — What you getting at?

HARRY — Ever thought you were a set-up?

JANET — Many a time…

HARRY — Part of a deal?

JANET — They wouldn't do that.

HARRY — 'They', had just committed an act of bloody horror, that sickened even 'them'. You were a hundred miles from the scene. That was the Crown evidence.

Oh yes conspiracy. You'd worn the beret, and marched. Guilt of association… but were you expendable?

Janet... you aren't capable of blowing anyone up... are you?

JANET — I tried making that point.

HARRY — But those who were... aren't here. Which may satisfy them. It may satisfy the RUC... MI5... the IRA... even the British public. It may even satisfy you... Janet you have been here fourteen years. Write it down...

JANET — In the beginning was a family, and a farm, and hedges that were tall and made a mystery of the fields... And Dundalk was full of horses. Tall, proud, and black-maned... and the horsemen were young, and sang wild songs.

HARRY — Write it down Janet, for Chris' sake... write it down...

JANET — But the radio said, 'There's another shot dead, and he died with a gun in his hand.' But nobody said why the man laid dead... he died for the love of his land.

My joy is cradled in the earth Harry. Don't make a cause of me. I am to be kept in stone. To live, day by day. Another fourteen years to get through... I can't allow myself to think about it...

HARRY — Martyrdom Janet! Prepares the same misery for those not yet born...

JANET — Leave me alone Harry... and let that child sleep who cannot say my name.

Fade out: Female Wing – Education Room.

◆ ◆ ◆ ◆ ◆

Male Prison Landing

Monitor(s): General activity.

Light up: ACKROYD. He sits in his bunk writing a letter. Two other cellmates asleep alongside.

ACKROYD

Dear Harry.

Well, here I am again. Sorry to have let you down, but I've made a mess of things... I couldn't manage outside... I tried but there's nowhere to go, nobody wants you, and it hurts.

It's rotten in here. We are threed up, and there's shit smeared all over. Even a turd on the toilet roll. Somebody's idea of a joke...

I know I done wrong again, but why they have to degrade you like this I cant understand.

Still I can cope with chokee! I know the ropes. I can survive in here. I'm back...

Yours

Billy Ackroyd

Fade out: Male Prison Landing.

◆◆◆◆◆

Female Wing – Education Room

Monitor(s): F.P.O. approaches screen and passes through.

Light up: JANET and HARRY.

HARRY — What is it about these bloody prisons… It's like he was relieved to be back. Bloody Hell Janet! How will the mould ever be broken if even those who are locked away… Know where they belong!

[*She passes him a slip of paper which he conceals just before the arrival of the F.P.O.*]

F.P.O — [*Enters*] Time sir! There's a message from the A.G. Will you call into the office?

Fade out: Female Wing – Education Room

◆ ◆ ◆ ◆ ◆

Assistant Governor's Office

Monitor(s): Cheerful and smiling uniformed staff.

Light up: New A.G. Nicholson and Mrs Gates ensconced.

Enter HARRY.

NICHOLSON — Come in… Mrs Gates I believe you know.

HARRY — Yes! I'm sorry… but I was expecting to see George.

NICHOLSON — Yes! Well let me introduce myself… Nicholson! I've taken over as A.G. on this wing.

HARRY — Oh!

NICHOLSON — Do have a seat…

HARRY — And George?

NICHOLSON — Transferred… It happens… Often quite suddenly in the prison service… Probably hadn't time to get in touch. Prisoners have a name for it… ghosting!

However I wanted this meeting… Tell me… Why are you still coming here, when you are not being paid?

Fade out: A.G.'s Office.

◆ ◆ ◆ ◆ ◆

Female Wing – Education Room

Monitor(s): Prison corridor.

Light up: JANET and HARRY.

JANET — There's a question!

HARRY — And where money is the token of honour, what's the answer?

Do I enjoy coming here?

JANET — They wouldn't find that credible.

HARRY — No! They don't come here for fun.

I said, 'You know how it is, the girls shout "So Long Harry, see you next Tuesday." Well, it's only a couple of hours out of my life. You begin a relationship… someone might be looking forward to seeing you… Maybe you've begun to build up someone's feeling of worth. You wouldn't want to destroy that. "Nice to have known you, but it's not worth my while coming now".'

JANET — That didn't convince them either! Truth is, you can't put your arms around the world Harry me old son. They are practical people… Give'm a practical answer.

Fade out: Female Wing – Education Room.

◆ ◆ ◆ ◆ ◆

Assistant Governor's Office

Monitor(s): Prison exterior.

Light up: HARRY, NICHOLSON, MRS GATES.

HARRY — To be honest Mr Nicholson.

NICHOLSON — Oh' yes! Let's be honest.

HARRY — It's a curious social situation. I mean, I find it fascinating. Being a writer myself, maybe one day, I'll have something to say about it…

NICHOLSON — Ah I see! [*A triumphant confirmation*] You are coming here for research. Well, I think the Home Office will take a different view of this…

HARRY — No! Look… I came to open up some hearts, and minds… To get them to write. To give them a voice… There'll be an anthology. Everything will be submitted.

MRS GATES — Hmm!

HARRY — I'm sorry Mrs Gates… did you say something?

But look, I can't close my own eyes and ears… I mean, am I some sort of a danger?

NICHOLSON — We expected you to stick by the rules.

HARRY — But I do…

NICHOLSON — [*NICHOLSON consults his report*] Sometimes you come from the gate by yourself…

HARRY — Eh? Well yes! If I'm the only one there. Or the other teachers go into the male wing… I'm not a security problem am I?

NICHOLSON — You approach prisoners on the wing.

HARRY — Like… 'Hello Susan?' 'How are you Bridget?' In passing. They are on the wing like on the pavement… Should I ignore them? Not say 'Hello Marty, are you feeling better?' You don't mean Marty? She was cleaning the floor. I said, 'Take care of yourself…' You don't mean that was reported?

NICHOLSON — You may not think it important…

HARRY — Come on! And have you told the padre? Does he know the risk he's running? Look, I'm very circumspect…

NICHOLSON Are you?

HARRY Don't you think so?

NICHOLSON You've left some books with the office, for handing out at Christmas.

HARRY That's right. I didn't seal them up. I know you have to examine parcels.

NICHOLSON We know they are books!

HARRY Of course. The dedications were the problem. How can you say, 'Merry Christmas' to someone in jail? Eh? I just put... 'Love, and Best Wishes, for Christmas' 'to Janet', 'to Bridget', 'to Pat', 'Marty'... well all the same...

Difficult isn't it?

NICHOLSON We've decided it isn't right!

HARRY I don't understand.

NICHOLSON We've decided it isn't right you should give them these books...

HARRY Really! But why? They are entitled to books...

NICHOLSON Yes! But not as a Christmas gift from a teacher.

HARRY You what?

NICHOLSON Oh I know what you are thinking. It's petty... it's unreasonable! But we believe it's right...

HARRY We?

NICHOLSON Yes! The Governor, and I…

HARRY 'God' Has abolished Christmas…!

Fade out: A.G.'s Office.

◆◆◆◆◆

Female Wing – Education Room

Monitor(s): Corridor.

Light up: HARRY rehearses an interview with G.O.D.

HARRY Look here 'God' No!

Excuse me 'God'… but…

Listen 'God'… There's something you've got to sort out… I wonder if you could spare me a little of your time…

[*Picks up the phone*] Put me through to 'God'.

Pardon?

Which one?

There is only one.

Alright!

The one who knows what's going on everywhere.

Thank you!

Hello Sir!

About those things done in your name!

You can't allow it! Christmas is in your best interest… With respect sir, a lot of people are suffering…

The what? The delegation of responsibility. Is that scripture?... Home Office guideline!

I know it's your great gift to life, but all this free will, is bringing you into disrepute. People can't handle it!

But sir!

You've intervened before!

The Red Sea!

Very well! I'm sorry! Yes! I know the balance! I've brought a lot on my own head.

Didn't get it right!

OK OK 'God! If you can't, you can't... Goodbye sir! [*Puts the phone down*]

Somebody somewhere, say something!

Fade out: Female Wing – Education Room.

◆ ◆ ◆ ◆ ◆

Prison Exterior – Night

Monitor(s): Exterior, lit up in the darkness.

Light up: M.P.O.

M.P.O. Up there! There he is! Bring the light.

[*A spotlight tracks MACDONALD who has escaped onto the roof*]

There! At the stack! Hold him!

MALE CONS (O.S.) On the roof! On the roof! Roof! Roof!

CON 1 (O.S.)	Who's on Alfie?
CON 2 (O.S.)	Macsi's on the roof.
M.P.O.	Get those bastards blanked out…
CON 1 (O.S.)	Go on Macsi! Decorate their nappers.
CON 2 (O.S.)	Give em a few tiles Macsi!…
M.P.O.	Get them on report! Where's he gone? He's moved! Don't lose'm. Pick him up! Come on MacDonald. Psycho tactics will do you no good. We don't have to go along. There he is! Hold him! By the vents! Come on lad! Down you come! Don't make it harder for yourself… We can leave you there 'til you are sick.
MACDONALD	You have labelled us vermin!
M.P.O.	MacDonald you are in enough trouble.
MACDONALD	We who occupy the roof… petition the Governor. We are no vermin!
M.P.O.	Who's with him? Is there somebody with him? Who's up there MacDonald?
MACDONALD	The great Spirit o' the Sky…
M.P.O.	Jesus!
MACDONALD	We eat your crumbs and drink from the gutters. We live wi' the snow, and the dead leaves… But we are no vermin!
M.P.O.	Who you talking to MacDonald?

MACDONALD — We are the company of the moon.

M.P.O. — He's away wi' the mixer.

MACDONALD — We are no vermin.

CON 1 (O.S.) — He's on aboot pigeons boss! He's protestin' aboot exterminatin' the pigeons!

M.P.O. — God! I'm bloody freezin'! Why the roof MacDonald?

CON 1 (O.S.) — A think he's doin' his bird boss!

M.P.O. — Pick that joker up on report!

Look MacDonald, would you like to see the chaplain?

[*Aside*] Somebody shake out Mick the Vic.

How about the Visiting Magistrate son? She's very sympathetic!

MacDonald! Are you listening?

MACDONALD — We can look down on you… we are no vermin.

M.P.O. — C'mon lad. Be reasonable. I'm friggin' perished.

MACDONALD — We are tattered and torn, and have endured the wind, and the rain, but we are no vermin!

M.P.O. — What's in a name lad? Come down and we'll talk it over!

MACDONALD — We are closer to the sun. We are no vermin… And all who die behind bars, we lift their souls unto the stars.

M.P.O.	Oh Christ! The shrink! Fetch the shrink!
	[*Tiles clatter down*] Not the demolition job son! It lets the heat out of the building…
	The shrink! Next to the VAT 69…
	Look son! Would ye like a blanket?
MACDONALD	Naw!
M.P.O.	Would you like us to get in touch with your family?
MACDONALD	Naw!
M.P.O.	How about a cup o' tea?
MACDONALD	Naw!
M.P.O.	Hot, strong and steamy wi' lashings o' sugar?
MACDONALD	Naw!
M.P.O.	What do you want MacDonald?
MACDONALD	If it's all the same to you. A wouldna mind cocoa…
M.P.O.	You bastard! You bastard!

Fade out: Prison Exterior.

◆ ◆ ◆ ◆ ◆

Female Wing – Education Room

Monitor(s): F.P.O.s on duty.

Light up: JANET, BRIDGET, PAT, talking to HARRY.

PAT — Great lump o' stone, stuck in the middle o' nowhere... 'Ere! If somebody said. 'Five o'clock everybody in the world shout 'elp loud as ye can.' Nobody's gonna 'ear us, are they? Nah! Ye gets born... ye fink 'Oo am I?' 'Where I come from?' You see all these other geezers driftin' around...

'Ere!', you say, 'What's this all about then?'

'I dunno! Don't arsk me! I just got sent 'ere.'

Nah! It's bound to send us all a bit dippy... I aint sayin' this is a moral argument for drugs... I just wish we was all like 'orses.

BRIDGET — Horses!

PAT — Yeh! 'orses! You remember 'orses. You worked wiv'm did'n ye Jan?

JANET — Yeh!

PAT — I don' mean them ones you see on the box. I mean real 'orses, what smell, an' enjoy a good shit...

BRIDGET — Wha' is this? Bleedin' Garden of Gethsemane or summfink...? Cheer Harry up. He's got gate fever... Tell'm about that boy on the roof Jan...

PAT — Yeh! Come on Jan. An the woolly mouse!

JANET — Yeh! Well... Poor Marty is in the strips down below... on solitary... Loss of privilege, loss of tobacco... Y'know! So I had this woolly mouse, an' I unravels it... ties a fag, and a match to the end, and lowers it down through the bars...

BRIDGET — Yeh an' she's reachin' out her winder to get it...

PAT — Yeh! An' a little message, 'We' luv ye Lorna'... all tied on... An' down the wall it goes...

JANET — 'Here'! Who's tellin' this?

PAT — Sorry Jan...

JANET — So this guy on the roof... he spots it don't he! An' he guides it down... Wee bit to the left... Up a wee bit. Bit mair to the right...

PAT — An' the bleedin' screws is going round the bend. 'Ooo! You talkin' to MacDonald. Somebody up there wiv you?' 'Cos they couldn't see!

JANET — Poor Marty. She never got the ciggie. Couldn't reach it, and when she snatched at it, it slipped off, and fluttered down into the yard... But this guy... directing the operation from the roof... what a scream...

BRIDGET — Nice that innit Harry... When people try to help each other... even in prison.

F.P.O. — [*Enters*] Time sir! Come on you girls...

CHORUS — Ah!

HARRY — [*Exultant*] Identity!

PAT — Y'what?...

HARRY	Don't you see? Listen it's just come to me… Identity!
F.P.O.	Come along!
HARRY	It's what you recover, when you tell your stories… When you write… You recover your lost identity… They must know that… Without it, you are manageable…
F.P.O.	Come on girls… onto the landing…
BRIDGET	What's it like in them Cheviot Hills Harry?
PAT	Be a lotta horses there is there?
HARRY	Sheep mostly.
PAT	In' that lovely. Still 'ave springtime an' lambs an' that?
BRIDGET	'Course they friggin' do. All that don' stop 'cos yor in here…
F.P.O.	Will you come along girls. Come on… Now!
HARRY	But will you remember? Write, and regain your identity… Don't' forget! Who you are!
PAT	Give ye an old con's advice Harry! When you get through the gate… never look back! [*She gives him a hug and a kiss*]
HARRY	Janet! You remain the enigma…
JANET	[*Whispers*] Quick… stick this up yor jumper… Read it when you get out…
HARRY	Janet…!

F.P.O.	Right you lot… that's it… On to your rooms… Move along… This way sir… See you to the gate…
JANET	Goodbye Harry…
HARRY	Bye! Give my love to Marty and all the others…
F.P.O.	Come along… come along… come along Control!
CONTROL	Control!
F.P.O.	Education staff leaving the wing… over!
CONTROL	Received…
F.P.O.	Your last night is it sir?
HARRY	Yes…
F.P.O.	Not be sorry.
HARRY	Wouldn't say that.
F.P.O.	Had your holidays?
HARRY	Not something I plan.
F.P.O.	Oh I do… A weeks time… Tenerife.
HARRY	Must be looking forward to it.
F.P.O.	Oh I am. Keeps you gee'd up…
HARRY	I'm sure.

F.P.O. It's the looking forward to it. We all need that don't we? Having something to look forward to…

CONTROL G. Unit… G. Cac's on!

F.P.O. Thank you control.

HARRY Cac's on?

F.P.O. Computer speak for banging up. Central Automatic Control! The lights are going out…

HARRY Oh!

F.P.O. The lock will open shortly…

HARRY Good!

F.P.O. I think you've dropped something sir.

HARRY Oh! just a note I was making…

F.P.O. [*Retrieves it*] There you are sir…

HARRY Must have slipped my folder… Thank you…

Fade out: Female Wing – Education Room.

◆ ◆ ◆ ◆ ◆

The Apron Stage

Monitor(s): Blank.

HARRY

[*Pauses to read JANET's note*] A poem for Harry…

Make not a cause of me…

JANET

[*Light up: JANET talking over at a distance in her cell*]

Though all my days
Are kept in stone,
A land betrayed me,
With welcoming brown eyes,
And the tossed manes of horses,
Comforting to the touch.

What compels our loving,
Makes victims of us all.
But for an act of cruelty,
A bewildered people
Have walled me up
With yesterday's children.
Knowing no other way
Of repudiating…
Madness! [*Fade out JANET*]

HARRY

[HARRY pulls his collar up against the night. Begins to leave. Stops. Looks up at the sky, accusingly points a finger] Do you ever wonder if you've got the balance right? [*Exit*]

THE END

Long Shadows

Tom Hadaway and Pauline Hadaway

Written by Tom and his daughter Pauline Hadaway, this play was first performed in 1993 by The Live Theatre Company in their theatre on the Quayside in Newcastle.

Original Cast

Eve Bland	Jan Hirst Una Aunt Maryam
Colin MacLachlin	A Sinister Man Stellios Victor Nussenbaum Brigadier Yacob
Sharon Kennet	Khloud Nasyr
Derek Walmsley	Alec Butros Nasyr
Pauline Moriarty	Irene Nussenbaum Um Butros
Chris Karallis	David Nussenbaum Dimitri

Directed by Max Roberts

Characters

JAN HIRST	A freelance journalist, Haifa Israel
A SINISTER MAN	Secret Service Agent for Mossad
KHLOUD NASYR	An Arab student living in Haifa
ALEC	A plumber from Hartlepool
STELLIOS	A Cypriot prison officer
VICTOR NUSSENBAUM	A Jewish business man living in Haifa
IRENE NUSSENBAUM	Victor's wife
DAVID NUSSENBAUM	Victor and Irene's son, an Israel Defense Forces (IDF) conscript living in Haifa
AUNT MARYAM	Aunt of Khloud
UM BUTROS	Mother of Khloud, living in Nablus
BUTROS NASYR	Son of Butros, Khloud's brother, an agricultural worker from Nablus
UNA	American immigrant to Israel, living in Haifa
BRIGADIER YACOB	IDF Officer
DIMITRI	A negotiator, Palestine Liberation Organisation (PLO) middleman

Minor Characters

A woman from Sabra Refugee camp

Lebanese militiamen

IDF soldiers

Act One

1993 A Busy Street in Nicosia, Cyprus

JAN enters. Anxious, pacing up and down. Consults her watch. Growing impatient. Decides to wait no longer. Begins to leave. Confronted by the SINISTER MAN. Lowering his paper, coming from his seat at a café table.

JAN There you are!

SINISTER MAN You ready?

JAN Am I ready? What is this? Part of the discipline? Enjoy it, do you? How long have you been over there? Sat watching me, were you?

SINISTER MAN There was never any need to get involved.

JAN What the hell you saying? I am involved.

SINISTER MAN You know the background.

JAN I was part of it. I was there.

SINISTER MAN Of course you were. Then you know what he is. What he did.

JAN Sure. The man's an evil bastard. Give me a gun.

SINISTER MAN I believe you could. It's not what they want. Stick to what you do best. [*Moves*] Dimitri is probably waiting.

JAN I resent being taken for granted.

SINISTER MAN There were unanswered questions. Come on! Who knows, you might get a book out of it. As a journalist, isn't sudden death your bread and butter?

JAN Listen! By the time it makes a headline, even sudden death can be irrelevant.

SINISTER MAN You heard the shot. You were there when they brought him out. Close enough to touch him.

JAN Sure, I could've got it second-hand. At the Press Club, the official brief, or a double whiskey to a gob shite. But no! Not me! The 3 a.m. idiot! Frozen! Why is it always 3 a.m.? You know, somewhere I read, death really takes off at 3 a.m. Is that true?

[*SINISTER MAN only half listening. Looking for a taxi*]

SINISTER MAN What I like about Cyprus, at 3 a.m. you can get a drink.

JAN My boss, he insisted, 'Be there! Real understanding only comes from direct experience.' You know, I had to get my kid out of bed that night, and over to her Gran's. She was eight years old. Two days before I saw her again. And what does she say? Hallo, mum. How are you, mum? Glad you're back, mum…? No! 'Mum, you forgot to pack my gym shoes. I hate you.' Why are kids so unforgiving?

SINISTER MAN Because they are always being disappointed. [*He signals his contact*] There's Dimitri now! You ready?

JAN — Sure.

SINISTER MAN — No second thought? Good! Feel proud. This is for your people.

[*They leave*]

◆ ◆ ◆ ◆ ◆

Central Prison in Nicosia, Cyprus

ALEC sits reading in his cell. Enter STELLIOS, the prison guard.

STELLIOS — Hey, Alec! You got a visitor.

[*No response*]

A lady! Aren't you interested?

[*No response*]

She's got credentials. Mr Dimitri says, okay. He's a good lawyer. You should listen to him.

ALEC — How much she pay him?

STELLIOS — That's an insult to Cyprus. And anyway that's his business. Okay, maybe you got something better to do.

[*ALEC signs a resigned agreement. STELLIOS leaves, returns with JAN*]

JAN — Hi! Jan Hirst! Associated Press. [*JAN extends her hand. ALEC refuses it*]

ALEC — Right Stellios. That's your card marked.

JAN — Come on! Maybe a friendly journalist will do you more good than a lawyer.

ALEC Who says?

JAN Your lawyer. Mr Dimitri. Ah! So you can still laugh!

ALEC Friendly journalist! There's a novelty.

JAN We have met.

ALEC Yeah?

JAN [*JAN takes out a red Kaffiyeh scarf from her case and passes it to ALEC. He studies it*] Eight years ago. They were bringing you out. The soldier snatched it from your head. Threw it to the ground. I picked it up. Your blond hair, it surprised me. I shouted, 'Hey! You're not a Palestinian!' You probably don't remember. The police sirens, the arc lights, the pushing and shoving cameras…

ALEC They were all shouting. 'Who are you? Turn this way. What has happened to the Israeli? Is he alive?'

JAN Now we know all that. And he was dead. At the time, all that mattered was making the deadline. You know, grabbing the here and now. Not asking why. So, what happened?

ALEC Eh?

JAN To the Israeli. What really happened?

ALEC He was judged.

JAN I don't know why it surprised me. You being British.

ALEC What's surprising? People are surprising.

JAN Young men, you do it all the time. Get mixed up in other people's fights. But why? Money, adventure, romance, conscience…?

ALEC Had a problem, did you?

JAN What about the girl?

ALEC What about her?

JAN [*Taking out a notebook*] Khloud Nasyr. Origin Israel.

ALEC You spelt it wrong. Just another Arab name.

JAN Did I? How do you know?

ALEC I read your account. I read the Observer. Okay? So I'm a moron. [*He pushes the scarf back across the table*]

JAN Isn't it important to you? I wanted to return it.

ALEC Took you long enough. No. Finders keepers.

JAN She only got three years.

ALEC That's right.

JAN She served two.

ALEC That's right.

JAN Why?

ALEC How would I know?

JAN And the reduced charge?

ALEC So what? Conspiracy to murder. Accessory to murder. What's the difference? They do deals.

JAN There was only one gun.

ALEC What do you want? Short of copy? Kurds out of fashion?

JAN I have a job to do.

ALEC You wouldn't get it right. You never do.

JAN Her place of origin, Israel. Did we get that right? She was an Israeli Arab?

ALEC You mean, Palestinian?

JAN Only a word. It doesn't matter.

ALEC Is it a problem for you?

JAN Not at all. Palestinian. Palestine. Is that where it all began?

ALEC Cradle of history…

◆ ◆ ◆ ◆ ◆

1981 A Living Room in Haifa, Israel

IRENE brushes her son's army jacket. Victor is writing at a desk.

IRENE — Victor, without me you are a clock with no spring.

[*Calling off*] David!

VICTOR — Listen, Irene...

IRENE — Why don't you call Benny?

VICTOR — In the middle of the night?

IRENE — It's only ten o'clock New York time.

VICTOR — Israeli time, New York time? I ring Benny we both lose sleep.

IRENE — He has something important to tell you.

VICTOR — For once, Irene, let me do something on my own.

IRENE — What do you know?

VICTOR — I know we should have stayed in Finsbury Park. I know I should never listen to your cousin Benny.

IRENE — Always looking for someone to blame.

[*DAVID enters dressed in T-shirt and jeans*]

IRENE — David! Why don't you wear your uniform?

DAVID — Ma!

VICTOR She wants to create an impression on the neighbours. Next time you're home, son, bring the tank.

IRENE [*Embracing her son*] Aren't you proud of him?

VICTOR I am proud of him. What time is Khloud coming? Bring her for a meal.

DAVID We're going to Abu Yussef's.

IRENE You eat there? That place! Full of pimps.

VICTOR Mother, the Sixth Fleet is at sea.

IRENE Go to Hadar. It's more respectable.

VICTOR Then bring her home. She cheers us up.

DAVID Got to dash! Shalom! Mam! Dad! [*Gives his mother a kiss. Leaves*]

IRENE You encourage it, and you know there is no future.

VICTOR It's their future. They're young. There'll find their own way. Don't you want him to be happy?

IRENE Of course I want him to be happy. I'm his mother.

VICTOR Irene, she's a lovely girl.

IRENE That's got nothing to do with it. She isn't right for him.

◆ ◆ ◆ ◆ ◆

The Living Room in Maryam's Flat in Haifa

AUNT MARYAM reading. Waiting. Enter KHLOUD. She is wearing western dress. Surprising and embracing her Aunt.

AUNT MARYAM Khloud! Ah, going to see Daoud, eh?

KHLOUD Going to see David.

AUNTY MARYAM Daoud. David. Either way is a nice name.

KHLOUD And how do you know I am going to see him?

AUNT MARYAM The way you kiss me. I get a little share… Have you eaten?

KHLOUD [*Struggling with her hair*] Don't worry I get something out.

AUNT MARYAM Sandwiches. All you students live on. I suppose it's enough when you are in love. [*Takes over grooming Khloud's hair*] Here let me do that. Now, when are you going to see your mother?

KHLOUD Oh Aunty Maryam.

AUNT MARYAM I don't ask much of you, Khloud. You know it is impossible for her to come here. Please! She misses you. Speak to David… A mother is a mother, Khloud, no matter what.

◆ ◆ ◆ ◆ ◆

Victor's Living Room (as before)

VICTOR — [*VICTOR on the phone*] Benny, will you let me say something… please! Yes, Benny, you were right… the Syrians…yes… They did. And how do you know these things, Benny and President Regan don't?

IRENE — [*Cutting in*] Because he talks to Rabbi Kahane!

VICTOR — [*To Irene*] Rabbi Kahane? I thought he only talked to God.

IRENE — Exactly.

VICTOR — [*To phone*] Buy a villa in Cyprus! Benny, I'll do it! But I'm asking myself why.

IRENE — You should be grateful he tells you privately.

VICTOR — [*Hand over phone*] With such a mouth as Benny's, what's private?

[*To phone*] Sure, it's a big market… I know, we're surrounded by Arabs… but Benny, I make bathing costumes… 'Made in Cyprus'. Yeah, I already do that, Benny. I import the labels… So what are we on this planet for? You think we're going to be here forever? I know, there's David. … Yes, he's fine… We should leave our children property?

Benny, you are very smart, you have important contacts. You have really made it. What I can't understand, why are you always planning to move?… okay, Benny. Okay… I'll keep in touch… yes, Benny… One and a half million tourists need somewhere to go… yes… Cyprus…

IRENE — He's right. Where's the sunshine in December?

VICTOR — Irene, you want to talk?

IRENE — No. I want you to listen.

VICTOR — You're right. Benny… okay… goodbye… bye. [*Downs phone*]

Irene, whose Promised Land, eh? What was wrong with Finsbury Park?

◆ ◆ ◆ ◆ ◆

A Park in Haifa

KHLOUD — David, it's three hours to Nablus.

DAVID — It's your family. Go and see them.

KHLOUD — You don't know what they're like. We always end up quarrelling.

DAVID — Your mother…

KHLOUD — She clings to the past. I'm not like the village girls. Everything is *haram*. Shameful. Stupid. Afraid of their husbands. I don't mind putting a scarf over my head. But nothing will make me wear the *jilbaab*. I want to travel, be myself. I'm not going to change.

Their only principle is you must repay what you have been given. Okay! I accept that! Aunty Maryam brought me up. My loyalty is here.

DAVID — Khloud! Go and see them. It's no big deal. Hey, maybe I could come.

KHLOUD — You crazy?

[*They exit*]

◆ ◆ ◆ ◆ ◆

The Occupied Territories in Nablus

Home of UM BUTROS, mother of BUTROS.

KHLOUD — Come on, yamma, let's take our coffee outside.

UM BUTROS — In the alley?

KHLOUD — It's not so terrible.

UM BUTROS — No shade, flies, strangers staring. In Haifa we had ten rooms. In Beit Nuba a mansion! Orchards, apricots, melons. Now, I haven't enough land to dig my grave.

KHLOUD — Yamma! You're forgetting all the hard work in the fields.

UM BUTROS — Your poor father. His children scattered.

KHLOUD — Yamma!

UM BUTROS — Only you and Butros left to me. Where is that boy? He knows you are here. Talk about something cheerful Khloud! How is Maryam? Still on the sugar almonds is she?

KHLOUD — Oh yes!

UM BUTROS: She'll never find herself a good man.

KHLOUD: Better off with sugar almonds. She still asks after Abu Ziad. 'He was so handsome!'

UM BUTROS: Ha! That's a good one.

KHLOUD: Does he still go into Jordan with his tomatoes?

UM BUTROS: Oh yes. But the Jews have put a big tax on crossing the bridge. Ha! Maryam should know this. His wife wanted to go with him. 'You're getting on now. I could help you with the work.' 'Never,' he says, 'we are better off saving the tax.' Truth is he has found another woman in Amman and she is waiting on the other side of the bridge with two children.

'Those bloody Jews!' his wife says, 'It's a disgrace having to pay to cross the Jordan.' 'Some things we have to accept', he says, 'let us be thankful for small mercies.'

[*They laugh*]

KHLOUD: Good to see you smile, yamma.

UM BUTROS: I'll smile longer at your wedding.

BUTROS: [*Enter BUTROS*] Marhabah! (*hi*).

KHLOUD: Marhabtain! (*hi to you*).

[*They embrace*]

UM BUTROS: Look at his long face! It's your sister. Where have you been?

BUTROS: Talking to Abu Salah.

UM BUTROS You're not going to start all that again!

BUTROS They've driven a tractor over his field. His wheat and barley crushed. He stood and wept. The army said he had broken the law by remaining. But the letter they sent was in Hebrew. How can he read it? And what law destroys crops and tells a man he may not farm his own land?

UM BUTROS Her home is in Haifa. She doesn't want to hear these things.

BUTROS We are not so lucky. Go to other houses and everyone is weeping. They've taken a father, they've taken a son. At night an explosion. What's this? They are blowing up another house. Shooting children in the street.

UM BUTROS Butros! Don't talk about these things.

BUTROS They are thieves and murderers.

KHLOUD They are not all like that.

UM BUTROS I am not listening. I am not listening to any more of this.

BUTROS [*To Khloud*] You have forgotten how your father died. You have forgotten the road from Beit Nuba.

UM BUTROS [*Covering her ears*] No. No.

KHLOUD Butros!

UM BUTROS Khloud! Hold me! I never wanted to part with you. What could I do?

KHLOUD [*Hugging her mother*] Why do you hurt her like this? How can you be so cruel?

BUTROS So that you can see the pain she always hides.

KHLOUD If things are so impossible here for you, leave.

BUTROS Who will care for her? And the others who hang on by a thread. Khloud, I don't want you to come back and be a refugee girl. But don't settle for crumbs. Education is a weapon. We lost our country because the Zionists were educated and we were not.

KHLOUD You don't understand, Butros. Things can never go back to what they were.

BUTROS Do you remember, the morning I got out of bed to climb the fig tree in my pyjamas? You were crying, 'Yamma will smack you, Butros, Yamma will smack you. Your pyjamas is a mess.' And I said, 'If you are quiet, I will take you next time.'

◆ ◆ ◆ ◆ ◆

1991 An Office in Nicosia

A secret meeting. SINISTER MAN looking through papers. JAN enters, takes a seat. He hands her an A4 envelope.

SINISTER MAN — Photographs. Courtesy of Nicosia Police Department.

JAN — [*JAN takes out a photograph*] Are you sure this is the right way?

SINISTER MAN — He has probably never been face to face with his action.

JAN — [*JAN inspects the back of the photograph*] No name. No file number.

SINISTER MAN — They're not crazy, they've jobs to keep. Fifty dollars. It's what I like about Cyprus. The service charges.

JAN — Conscience has its price tag?

SINISTER MAN — Bullet entry… back of the head. *[He leans over, pointing*] Hands tied. Horrific, eh? We need to know if he's honest.

JAN — Shall I take in a leather couch?

SINISTER MAN — Keep it simple. How people face reality is important. To our understanding. Those who deny it are usually full of shit.

JAN — Oh yes, I've met them I covered Sabra and Shatila.

SINISTER MAN — Yes. Of course, we know. That was madness.

JAN — That was a massacre.

SINISTER MAN	Something out of control.
JAN	No. The place was sealed off. By us. By our army.
SINISTER MAN	The Phalangists. They were drunk. Crazy.
JAN	We let them through. We were watching through binoculars. Those people were defenceless.
SINISTER MAN	Soldiers on the ground. How can they know what to do in such a situation?
JAN	The butchery was intended. They were killing everyone.
SINISTER MAN	War.
JAN	There are rules.
SINISTER MAN	There are orders. Lawful orders, unlawful orders. Soldiers become confused.
JAN	A woman with a bundle pleaded with me. 'Um Ahmed' I guess that was her name. I said, 'Are you Palestinian or Lebanese?' She was pushing the bundle at me. It was blood stained. I said, 'Look, I'm not a doctor.' Then this bastard tore it from her. 'What's this? Bitch? Give yourself to dogs? Baduck. Whore. Palestinian shit.' I said, 'Leave her.' Showed him my papers. 'Look! Al Hamishmar. Associated Press. Accredited. Defence Minister Sharon. What the hell are you doing?' 'The hell we are doing is your dirty work, comrade Israeli. Gemayal for Jesus Christ and Abraham!' It was obscene! The bodies piled on each other. As a Jew I felt ashamed.

[*SINISTER MAN turns his back*]

You're turning your back on me.

SINISTER MAN — It was madness

JAN — You must not turn your back on me. I'm sorry.

[*He faces her again*]

You get so angry. You forget to be scared. The stupid things you say. 'Are you Palestinian or Lebanese?' They'd asked her husband the same question before they shot him.

SINISTER MAN — The invasion of Lebanon was anchored in delusion.

JAN — The bundle was her one year old daughter, shot through the back of the head. Just like these pictures.

SINISTER MAN — Sharon! We warned him of Sabra and Shatila.

JAN — Two thousand seven hundred men, women, children, babies. And always we have to believe in the guilt of one man.

◆ ◆ ◆ ◆ ◆

Nicosia Prison

ALEC pacing the cell. Picks up a book. Turns towards the entrance of STELLIOS.

STELLIOS — Good morning! How you sleep? You look terrible. Hey, here's your book. *Animal Farm.*

ALEC — Two years you've had that, Stellios.

STELLIOS — Yeah. I couldn't get into it. It's for kids. Who cares what a horse thinks? You got any proper books.

ALEC — Help yourself.

STELLIOS — [*STELLIOS looks through the titles. Slyly*] She's at the gate.

[*ALEC rises*]

On your feet. Now you're interested. Ha?

ALEC — For a moron, Stellios, you're canny perceptive.

STELLIOS — Eh? Hey, look. I can fix it she comes straight to your room…

ALEC — Hawway! I've no tabs, Stellios. I can't afford your fees. It'll have to be the visiting room.

STELLIOS — I tell you. Your lady friend's loaded. She must have connections. [*Finding a book*] What's this? *Women in Love.* That's more like it. Alright, Alec? Is this one canny?

◆ ◆ ◆ ◆ ◆

Nicosia Prison, the Visiting Room

JAN sits. ALEC enters to take a position facing her.

JAN — Hello. [*Offering gifts. Cigarettes and a book. ALEC studies the book*] Edward Said. Do you like him?

ALEC — Writes well. Changes nothing.

JAN — Do you write?

ALEC — Now and then.

JAN — Like to show me?

ALEC — Maybe. One day. When I get out.

JAN — When will that be?

ALEC — Who knows?

JAN — I understand they've given you a release date.

ALEC — Now who would tell you that?

JAN — Is it true?

ALEC — Would be between me and the Guv, wouldn't it?

JAN — Do you think about the future?

ALEC — Have I got one?

JAN — That's interesting.

ALEC — Look, I've been pissed about by you people before. You think you can buy my life with a book and a packet of fags?

JAN — No. I'm sure I can't?

ALEC — Well? [*JAN takes out the photographs. Hands them to him, studying his reaction*]

ALEC — There are many ways to kill people, only one involves physical death. [*Dispassionately handing back the photographs*] There was no malice.

[*She replaces them in the envelope*]

Conscience is a selective memory.

◆ ◆ ◆ ◆ ◆

1983 A Court Room in Tel Aviv.
The Kahane Enquiry

DAVID NUSSENBAUM in IDF uniform steps up to the stand.

DAVID — Lieutenant David Nussenbaum, sir! Israeli Defence Force. Commander 4th Brigade, 2nd Tank Division. I was two hundred metres from the first building of Sabra camp. I saw Phalangist soldiers taking men, women and children to the area of the stadium. I heard shots. I don't know what became of the people. I saw two Phalangist soldiers beating two young men, sometime between 8 and 9 a.m. the Saturday morning. They lead the boys back into the camp. I heard shots.

I saw a group of Phalangist soldiers kill five women and two infants. I went to report this via my communications set. My crew told me they had radioed the battalion commander. Always the same answer… 'We know! It is not to our liking. Don't interfere.'

◆ ◆ ◆ ◆ ◆

1991 Prison Visiting Room (as before)

ALEC — Always someone has to do the dirty work. Ask any soldier.

JAN — Choice or judgement?

ALEC — Rarely.

JAN — I'm interested in the psychology, the…motivation.

ALEC — That right?

JAN — But my boss would say, 'All they want to know is who fired the shot.'

ALEC — Keeping it simple.

JAN — Exactly. So, who fired the shot?

ALEC — Fuck you.

JAN — Sorry!

ALEC — I said, fuck you.

JAN — Tell me, does being rude come naturally, or do you have to work at it?

ALEC — It's no problem. All you need are the trigger words. Motivation. Psychology. Dirty work? Be honest, who are you mopping up for?

JAN — As a journalist?

ALEC — As a Jew. I'm right, aren't I? You are a Jew?

JAN — Would that bother you? Are you anti-semitic?

ALEC — Ask me what I'm against, but leave out the shit labelling.

JAN — So what are you against?

ALEC — People who belly ache. Judges who pass sentence, but let someone else carry out the execution…

JAN Met a few, have you?

ALEC Bloody sure. We are talking about half the human race…

JAN So, you just dislike people?

ALEC Fascinating. The way you put things. You've a nice style in answering your own questions. Well, sod your conjectures. It was the conclusion of many lives. Of dreams, anxieties, hopes. The sea, into which all little streams surrender.

◆ ◆ ◆ ◆ ◆

1983 Israeli Defence Force Barracks in Haifa

VICTOR walks with his son.

VICTOR David! Its like President Reagan says, 'All people must share our revulsion for Sabra, Shatila.'

DAVID So Shamir tells the enquiry he can't remember any report of a massacre and anyhow the matter doesn't bother him. How could he say such a thing?

VICTOR His mother and father died in the Holocaust. His whole family, they all died.

DAVID So he never has to feel ashamed?

VICTOR How would anyone feel? Look, they did not intend it to happen.

DAVID Dad, they requested bulldozers.

VICTOR They should have foreseen.

DAVID We supplied them. For mass graves. Like Auschwitz.

VICTOR But you spoke up, David. I was proud of you. You were honest. People respect that. Brigadier Jacob was proud of you. Go and speak to him before you decide anything.

DAVID It's my responsibility. I have to work it out.

VICTOR Your mother is looking forward to Cyprus. She needs a holiday.

DAVID Don't let me spoil it…

VICTOR Whatever you decide, you are my son!

[*They embrace*]

DAVID Take Khloud.

VICTOR What?

DAVID Khloud! Take her with you to Cyprus.

◆ ◆ ◆ ◆ ◆

Victor and Irene's Living Room

UNA enters and goes to admire the inscription above the door.

UNA [*Calling off*] Say! Irene! How old would this be?

IRENE (O.S.) What's that? [*Entering with coffee*] Oh that!

UNA It's beautiful.

IRENE It was part of the house.

UNA Guess you can't read Arabic.

IRENE Victor was for keeping it. He appreciates culture…

UNA Not like my Louis. 'Old things is bad memories. What for we should always be looking at relics.' That's why we got outta Miami!

IRENE Relics? In Miami?

UNA Sure. They sit around in wheelchairs.

IRENE No regrets?

UNA No way. Two other things wrong with Miami. Hispanics and blacks. Here I feel safe.

IRENE What you expected?

UNA Like coming home.

IRENE I know. Like that feeling you get walking into a house for the first time. Una! This house welcomed me. It was so comforting. Like it had been waiting. Like I was expected. Walking from room to room, opening each door. Knowing exactly what I was going to find. Isn't that strange? To know you belong. Una, this house put its arms around me. The feeling of love… it was beyond belief.

UNA Wow.

IRENE — You made a commitment, Una. You too believe, above all else you are a Jew.

UNA — [*Dubiously*] Yeah. [*With conviction*] Yeah! You know. I can't get over how small it is. But the roads are very good.

IRENE — I'm so glad you are happy here.

UNA — You bet. Thanks, Irene. I guess you and Victor will be looking forward to your holiday?

IRENE — Cyprus is beautiful. You know we have a property. A year ago, my cousin Benny fixed a deal.

UNA — A property?

IRENE — Oh, we are coming back. We aren't giving this up. David would never forgive us. Come on, I'll show you the garden…

[*They exit*]

◆ ◆ ◆ ◆ ◆

IDF Barracks in Haifa

BRIGADIER JACOB's office. DAVID enters. Salutes.

DAVID — Brigadier!

BRIGADIER JACOB — David! Come in! How are your parents?

DAVID — Fine, sir.

BRIGADIER JACOB — Good! Look, David, the Kahane Enquiry did you no harm. I speak for others. They said, 'There is the kind of honesty we can employ.' Sabra, Shatila! It was so sad. A shock to the judges. For centuries we are the victims and our humanity survives. Beirut was the loss of innocence. No longer the little David facing Goliath. We become a nation, we become like our persecutors. So we are not so special. Well great I say! We don't have to be better than everyone else. Wake up! Good morning! Welcome to the real world!

I was brought up a Zionist, David. My Uncle Simon, a wolf of Samson. Our great hero… Ben Gurion! Arabs to be regarded as human beings. We'd had peace with them before, we could again. But we have to accept life as it is David.

I want you to go to the base at Shalishut. They are interested in you. Listen to them. Hear them out. But don't run away. Don't break your mother's heart.

◆ ◆ ◆ ◆ ◆

Irene and Victor's Living Room (as before)

Enter IRENE and UNA. They are looking at holiday snaps.

UNA — I said to Louis, 'Louis', I said, 'We're going on the Heritage trail.'

IRENE — You got to Masada?

UNA — Naturally, we got to all the Biblical sites. It was so impressive. Imagine, two thousand years of sandals over that rough ground.

IRENE — And you got to the top?

UNA — Yeah, we took the cable car. Gee, that garrison of dead bodies, it was awesome. And somewheres else they was diggin' up. A bit off the beaten track. Not many go there… What's the name? The coach has to park outside the town on account of those crazies throwing stones… So you walk up the hill… Canaa! Yeah! That was it… there was a church built by the what y'may call'ems… Franciscans… on the spot of a previous church, built by the Crusaders… yeah! On top of a Byzantium church, and below that… get this Irene… a synagogue!

IRENE — Built at the time of the wedding of Canaa. So much is true. Did you see any Arabs?

UNA — Gee, Irene, you'd have to be blind not to see Arabs in Canaa!

IRENE — [*IRENE picks up a photo of David*] This is David with his C.O.

UNA — Oh! He looks so handsome…

VICTOR — [*Enters*] Hi!

UNA — Oh! Mr Nussenbaum, hello!

VICTOR — Mrs Stern!

UNA — Irene is just showing me. You must be so proud! He's really a good looking boy.

VICTOR Yeah. You settling in okay? How is your husband?

UNA Louis? Oh, he's fine, just fine.

VICTOR You like a drink, Mrs Stern?

UNA Victor… Mr Nussenbaum! I gotta be going. But thanks… you mind I bring Louis round to see these some day, Irene?

VICTOR We're anxious to meet him…

IRENE Why don't you take them? It'd be a reason to call back.

UNA [*Handing back the photographs*] Oh no! They're family. You should never let them out of your sight. [*Preparing to leave*]

VICTOR Anytime!

UNA Thank you. Bye!

IRENE I'll see you out.

[*They exit. VICTOR gives himself a drink. IRENE returns*]

IRENE Well, how was he?

VICTOR He says, we are not to worry. Go to Cyprus and enjoy our holiday. [*Touching IRENE by way of reassurance*] He's not going to do anything rash. Okay?

IRENE What about his leave?

VICTOR He's working on it. Oh! And Brigadier Jacob sends his regards…

IRENE — You know... they'll never forgive him.

◆ ◆ ◆ ◆ ◆

Aunt Maryam's Flat in Haifa

KHLOUD — Two years and she treats me like I don't exist.

AUNT MARYAM — She's a mother. No girl will be good enough for her son. Even if you were a Jew. Khloud! Have something of your own!

KHLOUD — Did you not expect to marry? If it had been for love?

AUNT MARYAM — It's no guarantee. How jealous we were of your mother when she made her great catch. A man with one hundred dunnums of land. Her life was lovely in the past. People were close, living, working together in the fields. Never out of the sound of each other's voices.

We would visit her, seeing her big handsome husband carrying the wheat and barley. She'd smile, slyly, catching our envy. Oh dear! Within ten years, everything gone. Poor Abu Butros! Take the land away from the peasant, and what is he? A crow! A gypsy! To be chased away. Better if she had shared his grave. Only your brother keeps her alive.

KHLOUD — What can I do, Aunty Maryam?

AUNT MARYAM — Get your degree. Be a doctor. The people will need you. Jew, Christian, Muslim, they all have pains.

◆ ◆ ◆ ◆ ◆

The Park in Haifa

DAVID in uniform.

DAVID — You should have heard him, Khloud! All this rubbish about the Wolves of Samson. You telling me they believe all that garbage? Eh? Well I'm not falling for that anymore.

KHLOUD — What would you tell your mother?

DAVID — What's she got to do with it? My mind is made up. Don't you see? Now I can come and meet your family.

KHLOUD — Are you mad? In their culture, girls don't take their boyfriends home.

DAVID — I wouldn't be going as your boyfriend… well you know what I mean…

KHLOUD — No I don't.

DAVID — Introduce me as a peace activist. Shalom Achshav!

KHLOUD — You are not thinking this through.

DAVID — What is there to think about? Until somebody makes the first move? Takes the first step?

KHLOUD I'm talking about you and me!

DAVID Don't you see? I can be free now. I can take you anywhere in the world.

◆ ◆ ◆ ◆ ◆

Irene and Victor's Living Room (as before)

VICTOR He wants her to join us.

IRENE Why?

VICTOR He's still in love with her.

IRENE Then he's a fool. She is only looking for a place in the street. I know how she feels. But she has to make up her mind. What she is. I know. Kids shouting at us across the road. Yid, Yid, Yid! I used to think, being like them would be better than being like me. Keep a low profile! Don't make a fuss! Hide! Pretend it's not happening. Even when they put me on the train at Frankfurt, and mother said, don't cry, Irene, it's only for a little while. Like a holiday, I knew. But they were under such pressure. Every week I wrote a letter. 'Dearest Mamma and Pappa, I have been a good girl today. Today I picked some English flowers for you.' When the war ended, there should have been some relief. Some news. But nothing. No letters came back. Everyone… gone.

[*VICTOR places a consoling arm around his wife*]

	The best thing you can give your children? Tell them the truth. Oh, let her come to Cyprus, if that's what he wants. But why should we kid ourselves? We are what we are, and the world is what it is. Simple as that.
	[*Smiles*] Ah Victor! You are so innocent.

◆ ◆ ◆ ◆ ◆

The House of Um Butros in Nablus

BUTROS and DAVID sit facing each other.

BUTROS	You claim to be a chosen people.
DAVID	No. Not me.
BUTROS	But I tell you. Rights are not a matter between God and man. But between man and his fellow man. What's the real reason for your being here?
DAVID	Friendship.
BUTROS	To the defeated? That we should accept our defeat?
DAVID	I say we should put aside our grievances in the interest of peace.
BUTROS	But lack of peace, Mr Nussenbaum, is the consequence of grievance. In 1947, your Mr Ben Gurion said, 'The Arabs own ninety four per cent of the land and the Jews only six per cent'. Yet in Partition you are given over half and we are called intransigent because we reject this.

DAVID Statistics!

BUTROS Oh! That's great! Dismiss the figures, until you and the lords of the United Nations have redrawn the map.

DAVID We love this land as much as you do.

BUTROS But not so much its peoples.

[*Enter KHLOUD and UM BUTROS carrying coffees*]

You aren't afraid to come here?

UM BUTROS He is a guest in this house. There is no need to fear.

DAVID Thank you. It's a big thing for an Israeli. We are afraid of everything.

KHLOUD Honest people can talk.

BUTROS Tell me, what is your relationship with my sister?

KHLOUD Butros!

DAVID It's alright. We were students together. Friends. We went to meetings. No more.

[*KHLOUD and UM BUTROS leave*]

Where I grew up, the schools were mixed, people from all over the world. Together.

BUTROS And where was that?

DAVID London.

BUTROS London? Here. Let me show you something. [*He produces a set of bound papers. Carefully unties them*] These are the deeds to my grandfather's house. You see? Assigned by His Excellency Bey Suliman.

DAVID Ottoman.

BUTROS And should we have no history? You British send Bey Suliman back to his villa in Istanbul, and should my father's home be up for grabs? Look. To Abu ben Nasr, his heirs, and assigns, forever. Whoever lives there now does so without this title.

DAVID My mother's family had a home in Frankurt. Their murderers sold it to pay for the cost of their execution.

BUTROS And for what you Europeans do to each other, my mother and father are to be put out of their home?

DAVID It was wrong.

BUTROS My father died on the road from Beit Nuba. Do you know where that is? Have you ever heard of it? No one in the world knows. So I am doomed to tell and re-tell the story out of the only memorial that remains. Which is here. [*He indicates his heart*]

DAVID I'm sorry.

BUTROS And how would you make amends, Mr Nussenbaum? Denounce it in some left-wing journal? And what is your compromise? How much can you give me back of what is mine?

DAVID First there must be peace.

BUTROS No, Mr Nussenbaum, first there must be justice. To take a man's house and say, can't we still be friends? That is to talk shit.

DAVID An honourable peace? Is that talking shit? When the alternative is the killing of children.

BUTROS You talk of killing children!

DAVID That is what I say to those who are prepared to wage all out war. All sides…

BUTROS Already you are waging all out war. Our children are killed and maimed by Israeli bombs. Delivered by Israeli jets. Only you have the means of all out war. Only you have the powerful allies to give you the weapons…

DAVID And PLO bombs in shops, buses and synagogues? A bomb in a carrier bag is every bit as deadly and vicious.

BUTROS You call trying to get back into your own house, an act of unforeseen aggression?

DAVID Then you endorse it? This PLO, Hezbollah, Hamas retribution?

BUTROS You are served by fear of all Arabs. It is of your own guilt. Of the night we will fall upon you with our long knives.

DAVID Arab terrorism! Which you would call Palestinian resistance!

BUTROS — Now you see it. So listen. Peace is not made between friends, but between enemies. Now go home, little Jew and think about that.

◆ ◆ ◆ ◆ ◆

1991 Alec's Cell in Nicosia Prison

STELLIOS — [*Returning a book*] What was this? Women in Love? It's two blokes rolling around on a rug! They're not fooling anybody! These books you get is terrible. What would your mother think? Reading books like this? [*Inspects another book*] *Palestine – the Road Back.* What's so special about Palestine, anyhow? Eh?

ALEC — Push off, Stellios.

STELLIOS — What about us? What about Cyprus? We got a Green Line. We got refugee camps. We got political prisoners. Who cares? What's the matter, my face don't fit? Sixteen year ago, I had a nice house in Famagusta. I wanna see it now, I gotta look through barbed wire. My wife made lace. She had a good business. We had prospects. We got married in St. Nicolas Cathedral. Today, it's a Mosque! Poor St. Nicolas. They still got him in there. Who cares? You don't even know who he is. He's Santa Claus. You think come here 'cos I've no one to talk to? Let me tell you something. I got loadsa friends. You got no friends. Okay. So we're both lonely. But I'm down for a pension. What are you down for? Put that in your pipe and smoke it.

Hey! You think I got all day, stand here arguing with you? I'm a busy man. I got responsibility. You miserable, bloody Englishman. It's everywhere you go, there's trouble.

◆ ◆ ◆ ◆ ◆

1983 Near the Ferry in Haifa

KHLOUD What's wrong, David? Don't let Butros get to you. I know what he's like. You think I haven't worked him out? Everything has to be the way he wants. Sometimes he drives me crazy. But he has been so hurt. Father was the same. He brought disaster on us. Beit Nuba! Mother told you about our mansion. She didn't tell you he hid an Egyptian commando there. There are many things you don't know, David. Hey, why don't we take the subway to Carmel? Go to the Sculpture Garden? Have a drink and listen to the guitars?

DAVID I have to be back at the barracks for seven.

KHLOUD Alright. We'll just sit and watch the ferry come in. Maybe you'd be better off not seeing me.

DAVID No.

KHLOUD Your dad wants me to go to Cyprus.

DAVID No. I told him to ask you.

KHLOUD I wouldn't dare tell my mother.

DAVID Have you heard from them?

KHLOUD Butros has written. There is some family matter.

DAVID Trouble?

KHLOUD Knowing him. Probably.

DAVID He's in trouble?

KHLOUD No more than usual.

DAVID Does he go much into Nablus? Who are his friends?

KHLOUD I don't want to talk about Butros. I want to go to Carmel. Yallabina! Let's go!

◆ ◆ ◆ ◆ ◆

Um Butros' Living Room in Nablus

UM BUTROS Jamal has asked for you and I have accepted him. He is a good man. He will look after you.

KHLOUD What are you talking about, yamma?

UM BUTROS I'm talking about your cousin Jamal. [*Hands her a photograph*] Here he is.

KHLOUD This is crazy. Who says he is my cousin? Does Butros know about this?

UM BUTROS He is an engineer. He is coming all the way from Kuwait.

KHLOUD — Well I didn't ask him to.

UM BUTROS — My dearest, a woman cannot manage alone.

KHLOUD — Look, he's wasting his time. I'm not looking for this sort of thing.

UM BUTROS — Please! He is a good man. He will take care of you. His heart is full of kindness to our family.

KHLOUD — What makes you think I would want him?

UM BUTROS — That's not very nice.

KHLOUD — Not very nice! It's not very nice of you! What makes you think I want to marry at all? How do you know I haven't already got a boyfriend? Do you think I'm just sitting waiting for him to come along? Not very nice? It's totally insulting.

◆ ◆ ◆ ◆ ◆

The Alley Outside Um Butros' House

BUTROS is tying the handle of a hoe. KHLOUD closes to him.

BUTROS — Marhaba!

KHLOUD — Don't marhaba me! You arranged this! [*Demonstrating the photograph*]

BUTROS — Poor Jamal. Are you going to break his heart?

KHLOUD — It is not funny.

BUTROS He is such a fool, but he means well. You musn't blame him or yamma. Hey! I think he has sent you a picture of his younger brother.

[*KHLOUD discards the photograph. BUTROS picks it up*]

KHLOUD It stinks of oil!

BUTROS He would not have beaten you.

KHLOUD Thank you very much!

BUTROS I would not have allowed him.

KHLOUD Hey! Don't play big brother head of the family with me.

BUTROS And how is your little, liberal Jew? Is that why poor Jamal is to be disappointed?

KHLOUD How dare you.

BUTROS Don't turn down one fool for another.

KHLOUD What gives you the right to interfere in my life?

BUTROS You know me. I am full of contradictions, the strongest of which is hope. Go your own way, Khloud. I wish I could. Tell me. What do you think it is like in London and New York?

KHLOUD Why?

BUTROS — One day, when you are a famous doctor you will go there. Then you can send for me to drive your Mercedes. You must get one with the upholstery in chamois leather or silk.

KHLOUD — Any particular colour?

BUTROS — Oh, blue, green, red. Anything you like. But it must have a telephone. [*Puts aside the hoe*] So many want to leave. So many want to stay. All wanting the same thing. Just a little space to be happy in. [*Untying the Kaffiyeh around his neck*] You will not forget me, Khloud? [*Places the red scarf around her neck*] Whenever you leave, part of me goes with you.

KHLOUD — [*Holding his hand to the scarf*] Part of me stays.

◆ ◆ ◆ ◆ ◆

Aunt Maryam's Flat in Haifa

KHLOUD — Aunty Maryam, she's bringing this photograph of a total stranger.

AUNT MARYAM — She thinks it's for the best. You didn't tell them about David?

KHLOUD — Do you think they didn't guess? I don't know what to do. Victor has asked me to join them in Cyprus.

AUNT MARYAM — What does David say?

KHLOUD — I think it's only because of him.

AUNT MARYAM What do you want?

KHLOUD To be someone in my own right.

AUNT MARYAM Then you've answered your own question.

KHLOUD I'll never get into Medical School here.

AUNT MARYAM Then go abroad. Go where there's no discrimination.

KHLOUD And where in the world might that be?

AUNT MARYAM You could ask them at the travel agency. Someone might have it on special offer. You know! For one week only.

KHLOUD What would I do without you, Aunty Maryam? [*Kisses her*]

AUNT MARYAM Darling! Keep knocking at the doors. I think some of them are just pretending not to be in.

◆ ◆ ◆ ◆ ◆

The House of Um Butros in Nablus

A dawn raid. Sound over. Hammering on the door. Soldiers shouting. The splintering of wood. BUTROS walks into the open, followed by his MOTHER, who is struggling to hold and restrain him.

UM BUTROS No Butros! No Butros. Stay with me. Don't go.

UM BUTROS We are innocent people. You must not do this! We harm no one. In the name of God, Leave us in peace! Have you no mothers?

Have you no child who sleeps? Butros! Butros! Stay with me!

SOLDIERS [V.O] Open up, you bastards! Butros Nasyr! Come out! Out! Out! Burn this shit-house down. We want you, Butros Nasyr. Cockroaches! Out! Out!

[*The banging grows to a crescendo and ends with a great splintering of wood and glass. A SOLDIER bursts into the room, thrusts an automatic rifle at BUTROS shielding his MOTHER. BUTROS rises, raises his arms. The SOLDIER fells him with the butt of his gun. Enter a SECOND SOLDIER, they drag BUTROS away*]

◆ ◆ ◆ ◆ ◆

The Home of Victor and Irene in Haifa. A Phone Box in the Street in Nablus

KHLOUD and VICTOR at respective phones.

KHLOUD I don't know anyone else I can turn to. Victor, please!

VICTOR Don't worry!

[*IRENE enters takes her place beside VICTOR*]

It's probably just a routine check. You know what they are like. But they are very careful to observe the rules. If Butros hasn't been engaged in any...

KHLOUD He is a good man! He is my brother! I know him! He speaks his mind. He gets angry. But he is sensitive…

VICTOR If he is innocent?

KHLOUD He has done nothing…

VICTOR Then he has nothing to fear. They are looking for terrorists only. They are intelligent people. As soon as the mistake is realised he will be sent home…

KHLOUD Please, Victor, you speak to them. Only if someone like you speaks out will they listen. Only someone like you can make them understand. Please!

VICTOR Khloud! Khloud, be calm. Who am I? I am just a little man. They are very busy…

KHLOUD They are your people. You are one of them. Please Victor, speak to them.

VICTOR Alright! Alright! There is someone I can speak to…

KHLOUD Please Victor!

VICTOR Sssh! I promise… there! Don't!

KHLOUD You are our only hope…

VICTOR Go home, and I'll see what I can do…

KHLOUD Now, Victor! Now! Do it now!

VICTOR I will. I will… I will do it right away. But I want you to go home. Khloud! Don't worry… who knows your family may already have good news!

KHLOUD Please, Victor!

VICTOR I promise. I promise… I will contact you… [*VICTOR replaces the phone… pauses. VICTOR picks up the phone and begins to dial. IRENE intervenes, cutting it off*]

IRENE Are you crazy? Isn't your son in enough trouble? What good will this do? How do you know he is not a terrorist? You've only got her word for it. Victor this puts us all in danger.

VICTOR It's her brother… Irene! She's desperate.

IRENE All the more reason for her to lie. All the more reason to fear her. Please Victor, think only of your son.

[*A moment's indecision and VICTOR replaces the phone*]

◆ ◆ ◆ ◆ ◆

The House of Um Butros in Nablus

Dark and empty.

LOUD HAILER (O.S.) Pay attention! Pay attention! On the order of the Director of Al Fara'a Detention Centre, you are to collect the body of the deceased prisoner, Butros Nasyr. The interment must take place between twenty one hundred hours and midnight. Only the Mukhtar and six close relatives may attend. There is to be no ceremony and no demonstration. Is this understood?

[*Enter KHLOUD carrying Butros' red kaffiyeh. UM BUTROS follows, carrying a burning torch*]

UM BUTROS All my loved ones gone! Now we are two women alone.

KHLOUD Yamma!

UM BUTROS You went to meet your life so full of hope. Now your brother's body mingles with the dirt.

KHLOUD Yamma, tell me what to do.

UM BUTROS I cannot bear to look at you, Khloud, you re-open my wounds. I am forsaken in a world without conscience. May their mothers suffer the same agony.

[*UM BUTROS leaves. KHLOUD kneels*]

◆ ◆ ◆ ◆ ◆

Aunt Maryam's Flat in Haifa

Kneeling, KHLOUD ties the red scarf around her neck. AUNT MARYAM approaches her.

KHLOUD They had arranged to put him in Jericho or Hebron and not in the cemetery of our family. But we refused and said, he must be in his father's grave. After negotiation, they replied they would give him to us. I uncovered his body and found the heart was opened.

AUNT MARYAM How do you mean, opened?

KHLOUD It's taken out. All his stomach and lungs were missing. Everything in the body space. [*Emotionally caught up. Comforted by MARYAM*] They forced me to cover him up again. The others were not allowed to see. Not even his face. We had brought lamps into the night. Just the six of us. We prayed over him.

AUNT MARYAM For this I blame myself. I sheltered you. You know, I used to listen to the speeches on Cairo Radio. Believing every word. They would come to our rescue. And after that dreadful war, all that mattered was holding this corner, taking care of you…

KHLOUD Alright, Aunty Maryam. I have no more tears.

AUNT MARYAM Then I thought… they will give us freedom… they'll give us a share. Because we are patient and enduring. Sumud! The Jews are here to stay. It's a miserable reality. I didn't choose to be an Israeli citizen. And I couldn't take you to a Palestinian homeland that didn't exist. How can I tell you to be compassionate? How can I tell you peace comes through forgiveness?

KHLOUD — Sometimes you refuse to believe that those who love you can betray you. But this I now know. I am not an Israeli. I am an Arab. Those who wish to live in peace must be taught justice.

◆ ◆ ◆ ◆ ◆

Irene and Victor's Living Room

IRENE — Victor! We have been over it fifty times! They were doing these things to each other before we came.

VICTOR — I might have done something…

IRENE — Filling their children's heads with lies. Teaching them to hate. Little children! They won't let go of the past. So these tragedies go on happening. Kill the Jews! Kill the Jews! I have been hearing that from the day I was born. We are fighting for our lives! What do you expect young soldiers to do? Some of them react. It's inevitable.

And that lot in Tunis, Amman, Damascus. What are they doing? Rubbing their hands. They don't care. More martyrs and laying the blame at our door! Arabs! They want us to love them. They don't even love each other. Well, I'm not having it, Victor! You have nothing to reproach yourself for. Whatever happened to her brother… What have you ever done, but show kindness?

◆ ◆ ◆ ◆ ◆

1993 The Visiting Room in Nicosia Prison

ALEC — This is the way nations are formed. Winners and losers.

JAN — But you went in with the losers?

ALEC — Already was one. Fully experienced.

JAN — So, as a drop out, you made some sort of romantic decision, to identify with the underdog.

ALEC — Romantic? I was born in Hartlepool.

JAN — But it wasn't your fight.

ALEC — Being evicted, being told your worthless isn't exactly confined to the Middle East.

JAN — Come off it, Alec!

ALEC — You're not saying I'm the only British lad come out here?

JAN — No. I'm not saying that.

ALEC — Started off with the Crusaders sailing from Redcar.

JAN — Redcar? Where's that?

ALEC — Good question. Plenty in Britain couldn't answer. Loads of lads come over here after me. Still coming. Difference being… I knew why.

JAN — There's arrogance. Thinking you can personally intervene in history.

ALEC Matches the arrogance of them that say 'Stay where you are and leave this to us.'

STELLIOS [*Enter STELLIOS with a jug and glass*] You thirsty, ma'am? Maybe you like an orange juice.

ALEC Oh aye! What's going on here? This prison is unbelievable.

STELLIOS This is Nicosia, Alec, not Wormwood bloody Scrubs! I'm a Greek. We have respect. Okay?

ALEC [*To JAN*] It's a bit off beat, y'know. See, I'm the biggest thing they've got.

JAN You're joking. They got an ex President in here.

[*To STELLIOS*] What about Nikos?

STELLIOS Nikos? There is a really great man. He kill hundreds.

JAN [*Accepting the glass*] Thank you.

STELLIOS A pleasure. Nikos? He is a real fighter! Hundreds! Turks! Brits! Colonial bastards! He kill them all! Not so much in here my prisoner, but my guest. [*STELLIOS leaving*]

ALEC Stellios! I've decided not to go out for a meal tonight. Could you bring me the menu and a wine list…

STELLIOS I'm a nice man, Alec, but you piss me about and I change.

◆ ◆ ◆ ◆ ◆

1983 Victor and Irene's Living Room in Haifa

VICTOR sampling a plate of sandwiches. Enter IRENE putting down a case. Anxious.

IRENE — Where are those children? Victor! You nearly ready? [*She checks the bags and luggage*] Don't you start eating that food. [*Begins to pack it away*]

VICTOR — What you got there?

IRENE — Something to keep us going. Cheese, turkey drumsticks, a little fruit...

VICTOR — One, two, three... Irene, there are ten bananas!

IRENE — Yeah and some grapes.

VICTOR — What's in the flask?

IRENE — Tomato soup with croutons.

VICTOR — Irene, it's an hour's flight...

IRENE — It won't be wasted. It gets shared round.

VICTOR — But the plane only carries a hundred people.

IRENE — You got your glasses? Taken your pill?

VICTOR — Yes.

IRENE — Tickets?

VICTOR — Why should I have the tickets?

IRENE — Because I gave them to you.

VICTOR [*Groping in his pockets*] I have not got the tickets.

IRENE What are you saying, Victor?

VICTOR I remember, you had the tickets…

IRENE Ten minutes ago, I gave you the tickets.

VICTOR Why should you give me the tickets?

IRENE Because you said I would lose them.

VICTOR Then I was right!

IRENE Inside pocket, Victor.

VICTOR Look I haven't got the tickets. I never had the tickets… I got the tickets! Irene! What would I do without you! Forgive me! Just I'm so excited! I love you! [*He embraces her*]

IRENE If you love me, give me the tickets.

VICTOR Are you happy?

IRENE Yeah.

VICTOR I'm going to give you a great holiday.

IRENE I know.

VICTOR I want you to be happy.

IRENE I am happy, Victor. I am happy.

UNA [*Enters*] Yoo hoo! There you are! I brought you something for the trip. It's only a date cake. Well, maybe you'll get peckish…

IRENE	Isn't that nice, Victor?
VICTOR	Yeah! Very thoughtful.
UNA	It's nothing.
IRENE	[*IRENE hands VICTOR the cake*] Put it in the case.
VICTOR	Sure I'll squeeze it in somewhere.
UNA	I wish I was going. I got the urge to travel again. I said to Louis, 'I'm practically a gypsy.' But he's putting down roots.
(O.S.)	[*A car horn*]
IRENE	That's the children. David's driving us to Ben Gurion.
VICTOR	[*Discovering something while putting the date cake into the case*] Hey, what's this? What we got here?
IRENE	Oh them…
VICTOR	There must be two hundered of them…
IRENE	The labels we can drop off at the workshop in Larnaca. On the way to the villa.
VICTOR	In my case. This is my case…
IRENE	[*By way of explanation to UNA*] We got an export license. Anyone would think we were breaking the law.
VICTOR	I'm not worried about breaking the law. I'm worried about the security checks. They go through everything.

IRENE — [*To UNA*] Just making up the baggage allowance.

VICTOR — What they gonna think? What kind of a man carries two hundred bikinis in his suitcase?

UNA — A lucky man.

VICTOR — That's right! That's what I am. I'm a lucky man. Look at her! Go on, look at her! Brains and beauty! Feast your eyes! What a woman! [*Takes IRENE in a great embrace*]

[*DAVID and KHLOUD enter*]

DAVID — Okay dad? You ready?

VICTOR — We're coming! Khloud, you look great. But are you okay? [*He presses her hand*]

UNA — I wanna take your picture. You all look so happy. Come on! Come on! [*Lining them up for a snap*]

VICTOR — You got your leave sorted alright, son? Eh?

DAVID — Yeah. I'll be over in a week.

VICTOR — Didn't I tell you? What did I tell you?

UNA — [*UNA ushers them all across the room*] No, I think it's better over here…

IRENE — [*To David*] I'll ring you tonight…

DAVID — I'll be at the barracks.

IRENE — Be sure and be in.

VICTOR — Mother! It's only a week and we'll be together.

UNA — [*Moving them all again*] Oh I know. The inscription! Under the inscription. Come on! Come on! That's it. Lovely… great… You ever found out what it says, Irene?

KHLOUD — [*Reads*] Al Dar Li Allah… This house belongs to God.

UNA — Gee. That's beautiful.

DAVID — We'll have to get our skates on…

UNA — Right, smile everybody… now hold it. [*The picture is taken*]

VICTOR — Good. Now come on everyone! David, you take that case.

UNA — Let me help.

[*They all leave, carrying the luggage. The voices trail off. IRENE returns and stands alone at the threshold. VICTOR returns*]

VICTOR — Irene? You coming? What is it?

IRENE — I don't know. I just feel… I've forgotten something…

VICTOR — Irene…

IRENE — Silly. [*She leaves. VICTOR takes a last look at the room. Exits*]

END OF FIRST ACT

Act Two

1993 Alec's Cell in Nicosia Prison

ALEC sleeping. Enter STELLIOS.

STELLIOS Hey! Come on! Wake up, wake up! Two letters for you. They are good letters. Cheer you up. Now listen don't fall asleep again. One is from your mother… Your Aunty Ethel in Gateshead is getting new curtains. Yeah! And she is knitting you a pullover. See, your life is being kept going for you. It's in four colours – red, black, green and white. Someone should tell her they're not going to let it through security. Hey, Alec! The bit I like best. Some guy in a fast food shop in the west end of some place, he is giving your old man free kebabs. What's the matter? Look, I'm sorry, it's my job I read your letters. Come on! It's full of kisses from your nieces and nephews, So you can't be such a bad man. Okay. You've been here nine years. But you only come once. For twenty years, I am having to come every day. Who is worst off? The other letter is from her.

[*ALEC swings out of his bunk, grabs the letter*]

Yeah she is sorry she has not been to see you for such a long time. I dunno, Alec. She has something on her mind that one.

◆ ◆ ◆ ◆ ◆

Nicosia Prison Visiting Room

JAN A plumber?

ALEC That's right.

JAN Reading Mazzini?

ALEC No. That was my mate, Dennis. Always quoting things. 'In the face of the tyrant shall rise the tyrannicide.' And seeing those pictures of Beirut, shells bursting into blocks of flats. Bodies everywhere. Women, children. Horses! You know! What harm had they done? And everybody saying 'That's disgusting! Poor bastards' but nowt getting done.

Jan! I was losing sleep, putting words and pictures together. I said to him, my mate Dennis, hey shut them fucking books, I'm away. You can believe in simple solutions, can't you? Like, I'm not having this and wading in. But it's not that simple. I've been reading ever since. 'Course I've got the time here. Joyce, Conrad, Oscar Wilde. My head's cracking.

JAN So you went to Athens, then Damascus, then...?

ALEC Tripoli.

JAN Libya?

ALEC The other one.

JAN Lebanon. And then into the PLO?

ALEC Right.

JAN	And they put a gun in your hand?
ALEC	Well, they weren't looking for plumbers. By the way, you never came last week. You said you were coming. You should know what it's like in prison, waiting for someone coming…
JAN	Would it bother you, Alec, to know you'd killed innocent people?
ALEC	That was it. Another of Dennis's little gems. 'Never mistake manifestation for reality.' Took a day or two working it out. Then I thought, by God he's right…

◆ ◆ ◆ ◆ ◆

1983 Haifa IDF Barracks

DAVID	There was this little questionnaire. You know, with the little boxes you tick for yes or no. 'Would you consider killing someone for your country as something negative?'
BRIGADIER JACOB	It's not the job of a soldier, determining guilt or innocence. You start asking questions like that, it bogs you down. Look, David, I know you are going through a bad time.
DAVID	Military intelligence is not Mossad?
BRIGADIER JACOB	Of course, they don't exist… officially, but we overlap.
DAVID	I am a soldier.

BRIGADIER JACOB We are a nation of soldiers. But a strong army does not guarantee safety. They were grateful to you. They cleaned up a nasty sore in Nablus. And yes, some deaths are a matter of regret. When you remove a cancer… People under attack have a right to defend themselves. [*Picking up a report*] Khloud Nasyr passed through Ben Gurion airport at 11 a.m.

DAVID She is nothing to them.

BRIGADIER JACOB But she is something to you. David our sole concern is the protection of Jewish people all over the world. The last thing we want is a conflict between beliefs and loyalties.

DAVID My mother and father…

BRIGADIER JACOB Are our responsibility. The villa will be under surveillance. By the way, it has an excellent view of the Harbour. Come on, David. Cyprus is the TNT route, the PLO are drifting back to Beirut in their hundreds. Maybe your girlfriend is clean. She might cross over. 'Yahalom' eh? Work for us. They want to know what you think. Tell them. What you really think. It might save all our lives.

◆ ◆ ◆ ◆ ◆

Nicosia Prison Visiting Room (as before)

ALEC — You ask me why? We were going back to save lives. For Christ sake, you were in Beirut after the massacres. Three years on, the survivors were under siege again. We're talking about old people, women, kids, left behind. Starving, reduced to eating cats and dogs, hunting through garbage. No water, no medicine, no electricity. Doctors amputating legs and arms of children by torchlight. Even the doctors and nurses being murdered. You read the testimony. It wasn't a sentimental journey to see old friends. We were going back to fight.

JAN — Hold on. We'd pulled out. That was the Amal siege. Arabs! Who are your friends?

ALEC — Who are the fucking enemies? The Americans had guaranteed those camps. The Amal were armed with M16s made in the USA. Oh, my enemy was clear. Israeli intelligence. Picking up our men trying to get back to defend wives and kids. Maybe they shouldn't have given me that job. Who'd want it? After so many defeats. Kicking our heels, demoralised, everything falling apart. It had crossed my mind. Time to get out. Had it all planned. Booked a flight. Written to my mam for the money. Then they pull your name out of a billycan…

JAN — How could you be sure you had the right man?

ALEC — Mossad had posted him to Cyprus. He was known on the West Bank. He'd put a hundred into Al Fara'a. You know – one of your torture factories. Well not yours personally…

JAN — So it was revenge?

ALEC — Nothing so sweet and simple. It was a trade. His life for theirs.

JAN — Had the girl supplied the information?

ALEC — My orders were clear. His name was Nussenbaum.

JAN — So how did you arrive?

ALEC — Easy. Just up to the door… and knocked.

◆ ◆ ◆ ◆ ◆

1983 A Villa in Larnaca Cyprus

(O.S.) — [*A knocking at the door*]

IRENE (O.S.) — Victor!

VICTOR (O.S.) — Okay. I'll get it.

[*Pause. Enter VICTOR preceding ALEC*]

VICTOR — Come through! Come through!

ALEC — Sorry to bother you. A kettle of water will do. I think the radiator has sprung a leak.

VICTOR — Sure. Step in. Going far?

ALEC — Trudos.

VICTOR — Lovely. [*Goes to fill kettle. ALEC cases the room*]

VICTOR (O.S.) Up the mountains, eh? Holiday?

ALEC Aye! My first time in Cyprus.

VICTOR (O.S.) That so? Like it?

ALEC Canny.

VICTOR (O.S.) Canny! I thought so! That accent. You are a Geordie, right?

ALEC What?

VICTOR [*Entering*] Newcastle?

ALEC Near enough.

[*Enter IRENE taking in the situation*]

VICTOR Hey, Irene! You'll never guess where this young man's from.

IRENE How do you do?

VICTOR We had an uncle in Jesmond.

ALEC Jesmond? Out of my class!

VICTOR Oh no. Not my old Uncle Matty. He pickled beetroot.

IRENE He did not. He manufactured car batteries.

VICTOR Only when he ran out of beetroot.

IRENE Rubbish! Everytime he tells it, it's different.

VICTOR It's true. Y'see he'd stocked up with this acetic acid. So much acetic acid, he was up to here. The war comes. No beetroot, no onions, nothing. Just all this acetic acid.

Lucky for Matty he's got brains. He makes batteries. Now for batteries it should be Sulphuric acid. So they aren't good batteries. In fact they are dreadful batteries. So what does he do? Every week in the Newcastle Journal he's advertising. 'The Canadian Army never complained about a Nussenbaum battery.' So they never bought one either! Who was to know? He sold hundreds.

ALEC Didn't anyone complain?

VICTOR There's a war on. People don't expect things to last. [*Hands over the kettle*] You're taking a chance.

ALEC Sorry?

VICTOR Going up the mountain with a dodgy radiator.

ALEC It's a hire car…

VICTOR What! Then phone and tell them.

ALEC I did. They're talking about two days from Pafos…

VICTOR What? That's crazy! They're crooks.

ALEC Okay. It was a cheap hire.

VICTOR Take it to a garage and charge 'em.

ALEC I think you're right. I got loads of time. But I use the car to sleep in. Thanks! [*Leaves*]

VICTOR Oh.

IRENE [*IRENE re-enters*] What was he saying?

VICTOR He sleeps in his car.

IRENE I might have known. If you ask me he probably stole it. Such people you attract.

VICTOR What's that supposed to mean?

IRENE It means we can kiss goodbye to the kettle.

VICTOR Irene.

IRENE Are you ready for the beach?

VICTOR We are going to the beach?

IRENE Yeah. I'm going to throw you off a cliff. What have I been saying all day?

VICTOR Let's go to the beach.

IRENE So now we're going.

VICTOR Just so as I know. Is Khloud coming?

IRENE You'll have to ask her. I'll get the towels. [*Leaves*] Pickled beetroots!

[*Enter KHLOUD with the kettle*]

VICTOR Irene wants to know, you coming to the beach. Khloud?

KHLOUD No. I'm waiting for a call from David.

VICTOR Oh sure. Ah! I see you got the kettle. Has he gone? Y'know! That young man lived right next to my Uncle Matty. Would you believe it!

KHLOUD He said to thank you.

[*IRENE returns ready for the beach*]

VICTOR Hey, Irene, you see! The kettle came back. He was okay. You know, my Uncle Matty always said that. Newcastle on Tyne. They was very nice people, but you had to get to know them… [*Going to the window*] I hope he gets where he's going.

IRENE Victor! Come on! Stop worrying about other people.

VICTOR Okay. Ready. See you later, Khloud. Tell David, tomorrow is all arranged.

◆ ◆ ◆ ◆ ◆

1993 Nicosia Prison Visiting Room

JAN [*Reading*] I stood with my back to the world. Eyes fixed on sea and sky. A blond couple walked up and down the beach hands clasped.

◆ ◆ ◆ ◆ ◆

1983 The Beach

ALEC — I said to them in my thoughts, appreciate one another. In September the sea is calm and flat in the evening but its restless depths work on the soul. I said to them in my thoughts, come back tomorrow. The minutes and hours charged with an awesome significance, every moment passing never to be compensated for. Time no longer mine to play with. To put aside for a rainy day. Somehow I had convinced myself the job was the least important thing in the world. Everything, even the small pebbles I chucked into the sea, precious beyond words. [*He throws a pebble*]

◆ ◆ ◆ ◆ ◆

1993 The Prison (as before)

JAN — Do you think that is how God feels?

ALEC — That's right. Blame God. Do you like it?

JAN — It's nice.

ALEC — Will I make a writer?

JAN — Is that important to you?

ALEC — I'd like them to know, there's another side to me.

[*JAN offers to return the poem*]

No. Keep it. I'd like you to keep it.

◆ ◆ ◆ ◆ ◆

1993 An Office in Nicosia

JAN hands over Alec's book of poems to the SINISTER MAN.

SINISTER MAN — Of course it is interesting, as all life is interesting, and we are patient people. But the past has no more value, other than it confirms our present intentions. Where it fails to do that it can be re-written. You know what we are looking for… The day, the time, the place. The resolution of a doubt.

JAN — What if the same people who seek our destruction might have loved us, if we had acted differently.

SINISTER MAN — Is of no account. We live with what we are bequeathed. So he was a mercenary. A good mercenary? Not acting for money, but out of belief. So, what's so special? You asking me to admire him? Look, go back, take your time. Don't let things like this cloud your view. [*Returns the poems*]

This man, this woman, this enigma. This who did what, is all that troubles us.

JAN — Perhaps we fear their love more than their hatred.

SINISTER MAN — Oh! Absolutely! I couldn't agree more.

◆ ◆ ◆ ◆ ◆

1983 The Villa in Larnaca

IRENE hesitant before KHLOUD.

IRENE — Victor, he takes so long. What a man.

[*KHLOUD about to leave*]

Khloud, look I think it is nice you stay home and cook the meal. Nice surprise when David comes in. We'll go to the airport and… Khloud! I'm sorry I made a fuss… [*Shouts*] Victor! What is keeping him?

[*KHLOUD again prepares to exit*]

Khloud, you thought any more about your studies?

KHLOUD — All the time.

IRENE — Any decisions?

KHLOUD — Aunty Maryam says, whatever happens I will have to go abroad.

IRENE — I think your Aunty Maryam is very wise. Khloud, I know you think I've been unsympathetic. Believe me, I grieved for you. Losing a brother is something I understand. You and Victor get on so well together. Yet we have more in common. Victor loved London, you know. I never did. People there never meant what they said. Good to see you… how long you staying? You and I are alike, Khloud. We are left to pick up the threads. If I've seemed remote you shouldn't think I don't respect you. Both of us are lonely. Pain is very secret. Sometimes it becomes the only thing you can depend on.

◆ ◆ ◆ ◆ ◆

1993 Nicosia Prison

STELLIOS Hey, Alec, who's the first man you shot?

ALEC Go home, Stellios.

STELLIOS Come on, be honest! I was a soldier. You tell me, I tell you.

ALEC First man I shot was a Palestinian.

STELLIOS That right? How come?

ALEC He was wearing a red arm band.

STELLIOS What were you wearing?

ALEC A green arm band. I hadn't counted on a civil war.

STELLIOS Who can work it out, Alec? When the killing starts.

ALEC Comes the night when you just want to get home with no bother, suddenly you're face to face with a man with no arm band. You see the futility.

STELLIOS I think you didn't join up to kill innocent people, Alec. Why should you come half way across the world, risk your life for that? You know, she is having problems weighing you up. Maybe you're the first honest man she met. Good for you! Never be afraid to speak the truth.

ALEC And who was the first man you shot, Stellios?

STELLIOS [*Leaving*] You crazy? I tell you that, what sort of trouble am I in…?

◆ ◆ ◆ ◆ ◆

1983 The Villa in Larnaca

Empty. The telephone ringing. KHLOUD enters. Followed by ALEC. She looks to him for guidance.

ALEC Don't be alarmed. Take the call.

KHLOUD [*Answers the phone*] Hello! Hello! [*The phone goes dead. KHLOUD replaces it*] They rang off.

ALEC No point worrying. It's all set up. Keep calm.

KHLOUD Where are we taking them?

ALEC Nowhere. This is a safe house.

KHLOUD What about the police?

ALEC Who's going to tell them?

KHLOUD Mossad.

ALEC No chance. They're Hoppers. Come over from Tel Aviv, do their job and hop back. Cyprus is where they don't show their face. They're more unpopular here than we are. No, if the police show up, someone's decided we are all expendable.

KHLOUD What happens next?

ALEC We wait.

◆ ◆ ◆ ◆ ◆

The Villa (as before)

VICTOR enters carrying a case.

VICTOR — Something smells good. Hey, Khloud we're back!

IRENE — [*Enter IRENE*] Victor! Let's go and get changed.

VICTOR — *Changed?*

[*Enter KHLOUD*]

Oh, changed. Yes of course. We're gonna get changed, Khloud.

[*IRENE exits*]

[*VICTOR stalling*] David. He's bringing in the cases. Look, I'm sure he wants to speak to you. Y'know… alone. So we'll just… [*Begins to exit, but still holding back*] Y'know, Khloud, David is like me. Not really any good at making decisions. I love him. He's a good boy. But sometimes I just gotta say, 'David, I wish you would…' Y'know… then of course I got Irene…

IRENE (V.O.) — Victor!

VICTOR — A woman who knows her own mind. Would you do me a favour, Khloud? Somehow he's stopped talking to me. I don't know what it is, I think something is on his mind. He'll tell you. If there's anything I can do. You let me know. [*Closing to KHLOUD, he gives her a kiss*] [*Enter David. VICTOR exits*]

DAVID — What was he saying?

KHLOUD — Who?

DAVID — My father, what was he saying?

KHLOUD — He worries about you.

DAVID — I know. It makes me want to run.

KHLOUD — Are you alright?

DAVID — Something I want to tell you.

KHLOUD — Can't it wait?

DAVID — All the way here, I'm thinking of what it is. A decision. It's gone. Those little fish that swim out of your head. You should write everything down. Don't look so sad. It's not your fault. It's not anyone's fault.

KHLOUD — What is not our fault?

DAVID — I could never talk to them. It's the narrowness, like play acting. All the shoulds. You know. You should go to the culture centre. You should join the army. That's what I wanted to tell you. I need something more than the survival of a race. I can't give it words. Something nagging… suddenly I realised we didn't belong. That fundamentally was the trouble… they are absolutely right in everything they say, but it's not for us… Intellectually, I have no regrets. It's this fixation with the past. I go to your brother to offer peace and he threatens to kill me. That's crazy! To waste our lives nursing such grievance. Well I see everything clearly now. We get out, Khloud. You and I, to London.

[*KHLOUD looks beyond him to ALEC who enters with the gun*]

KHLOUD — You are never seeing anything clearly, David. Always you were looking at me without seeing. Now I am more than someone's object, passively in front of you.

[*David turns to follow her gaze. ALEC presents the gun*]

ALEC — Keep facing this way. [*ALEC throws a hood to KHLOUD*]

DAVID — My mother!

[*She pulls it over David's head. ALEC moves to fix the handcuffs*]

ALEC — You mean nothing to me. Just pray you mean something to those who sent you. [*Thrusts David to a prostrate face down position*]

[*To KHLOUD*] Call them down!

[*Goes to the phone. Dials*] Dimitri! It's in place!

◆ ◆ ◆ ◆ ◆

1993 Nicosia Prison Visiting Room

ALEC — [*ALEC closes to JAN*] You take a captive and close a trap upon yourself. Like the whole of life, we were all inside. Waiting for someone outside to say, 'It's alright. We've come to our senses.' Those not yet born have been calling out, spare us. So, it's over. We can all go home now. How much silence can you endure? Maybe the trap is all that's left. The whole of existence.

Maybe there's no one outside, or they don't know we're here. Or they've given up and gone away. Things begin to crumble with the thought, this will go on for a thousand years.

[JAN begins to leave]

Jan! for Christ's sake? What else do you need to know?

◆ ◆ ◆ ◆ ◆

1993 An Office in Nicosia

SINISTER MAN — He's right. The complicity of the Arab girl is clear. So who fired the shot is matter less. Forgive me saying, but you are in danger of becoming voyeuristic. Besides if you are unable to come up with the release date, it's not so important. Others can follow it up. Either way he is a dead man…

JAN — Why go on with it?

SINISTER MAN — It's expected of me.

JAN — I like to be straight in my mind. Don't you ever have doubts?

SINISTER MAN — No. my predecessor was always having them. He fell out of a train.

JAN — Isn't there any other job you'd rather do?

SINISTER MAN — Bee keeping. It fascinates me. Don't know why.

JAN — Why did they choose me?

SINISTER MAN — [*Opening a file*] Janet Hirst. Sabra... native born... Mother Elspeth Miriam. Ex Vienna, arrived Haifa, October 12 1947. Widowed, pregnant, stateless. One daughter. Margarete. By the way, how is she?

JAN — With her father. She gets married next month. All of a sudden she remembers she has a mother.

SINISTER MAN — Naturally. And where will they live? The newlyweds?

JAN — Tekohah.

SINISTER MAN — A settlement. How brave! How sad! Always to live behind wire and her husband carrying a gun. You are committed Jan. They know that. They have always known it. Sometimes they are mistaken.

◆ ◆ ◆ ◆ ◆

1983 The Villa in Larnaca

An empty room. The phone rings. Enter ALEC. He picks up and listens.

ALEC — Yes! Yes, alive and well. I'll give you the proof. [*Calling off*] Bring the woman!

[*Enter KHLOUD propelling IRENE to the phone. She is hooded and bound. ALEC removes the hood, strips the sticking tape from her mouth and holds the phone against her ear*]

ALEC [*To the phone*] Speak!

IRENE Benny! Oh Benny! For God's sake! Help us! Yes, we are all alive! Please, Benny! What is it they want?

[*ALEC pulls the phone from her. ALEC and KHLOUD struggle with IRENE and replace the sticking tape and hood*]

ALEC [*Into the phone*] Alright! Now you move it… … how long is that gonna take?… Don't give me all that shit! We want them all. You've got the list… Give us what we want. Or you're bringing your people out of here in bags… Yeah? Hey Benny! You're the Goldfish. The fixer! You dropped them in it. Let's see how much they're worth to you.

[*KHLOUD bundles IRENE out*]

◆ ◆ ◆ ◆ ◆

1993 Nicosia Prison Visiting Room

ALEC and JAN face each other.

JAN We are talking about the value of human life.

ALEC There's a scale? Like, kill one, two, three, you're an assassin. Kill two hundred thousand, big league! You're a hero! You get a victory parade!

JAN Come off it, Alec! That's crap! Face to face with a helpless victim. That's murder.

ALEC That's something, isn't it? Eh? Face to face. Not like sitting, pushing a button, dropping a cluster-bomb on a thousand refugees and fucking off at a thousand miles an hour. That what you mean?

JAN You had a choice.

ALEC Or should we just watch it on the telly? And if conscience plays you up, you can always go up to the Monument and hand out some leaflets. As long as it isn't raining.

JAN Don't be so self-righteous. Who the hell are you, to act as judge, jury and executioner? You're talking to me about prisoners and deaths in custody! You're no better than the people you condemn. Be honest. You couldn't cope. You made the wrong choice.

ALEC What choice?

JAN What about mercy?

ALEC Mercy? Fuck me, Jan! When they think that's an option in goes the boot. Know what they call it? Burning the agent.

◆ ◆ ◆ ◆ ◆

1983 The Villa in Larnaca (as before)

(O.S.) A police siren. Noise of helicopters overhead. A beam of white light floods the room.

ALEC throws himself to the floor, crawls under the window. KHLOUD follows.

ALEC — Get them back! Khloud! Keep down! [*KHLOUD crouches down. ALEC breaks the window with his gun. Screams*] You out there? Dimitri? Eh? You two faced bastard! Now we're all dead!

◆ ◆ ◆ ◆ ◆

1993 Alec's Cell in Nicosia Prison

STELLIOS — Hey, Alec, what you hoping to find in these books? You should know, life tells you more than books.

ALEC — Books are a record of life.

STELLIOS — Now you listen to me. They put anything in these books. They don't like the life they see? They write the book different.

ALEC — There are books and books…

STELLIOS — It's what I'm saying. And who is telling the difference? You want to sort out problems, listen to my wife. Books is about problems that was around before they wrote the books. Where's the books that's writing about problems that hasn't happened until after the book is written? You get me? Otherwise, you explain to me, how it's always the next day, I am thinking what it is

I should have said in an argument? Only a woman can do that.

The trouble is words. Now I know your mother is a nice lady, 'cos I'm reading your letters for which I apologise. Oh! By the way... [*Belatedly handing over a letter*] ...Some stupid newspaper is calling her the 'terrorist mum' ... but she says that's okay, 'cos the neighbours still call her Rose. Okay, so your mum's got good neighbours. But you see, when people really know, they can make up their own minds. This is the difference between real life and books.

◆ ◆ ◆ ◆ ◆

1983 Outside the Villa in Larnaca

Drone of helicopters overhead. DIMITRI stands at a distance. Shouting. ALEC has him covered from the window.

ALEC — Far enough, Dimitri!

DIMITRI — Okay! Okay, Alec!

ALEC — You burnt us, you bastards!

DIMITRI — Not us, Alec! Not us! Listen! There's still a chance. But we gotta prove something.

ALEC — There's only one deal!

DIMITRI — They don't want to talk! Only to Tunis! But Tunis isn't talking! It's a fucking mess, Alec!

ALEC — You make 'em listen!

DIMITRI — You gotta give me something.

ALEC — No Mossad property. No fuckin' way Dimitri! I've got good mates in that Israeli shit hole!

DIMITRI — Look! We got no ruck with the old folks. Give me the old people, Alec.

ALEC — Talk to Tunis!

DIMITRI — Tunis is backed out. I'm trying to tell you. You are not fucking listening. Nobody's claiming you. This is the end of the line.

ALEC — Push off Dimitri!

DIMITRI — Listen! Listen! Give me them! I tell you I gotta show I'm in control. For Jesus sake it's the only way. Keep the boy, but give me the old folk.

ALEC — Are you hearing this, Khloud? Do we go along?

DIMITRI — We've no choice! Alec!

ALEC — Right, you bastard! We'll give you them, but you better come up with a result. Khloud! Bring them out!

[*KHLOUD brings VICTOR and IRENE, bound and gagged. They push them out into the night*]

ALEC — [*Panics*] Keep low! Keep low! It's midnight, Dimitri! Tunis! Tel Aviv! They got to know! Time is running out! [*To KHLOUD*] I said, keep down. The bastards! We gotta go along!

◆ ◆ ◆ ◆ ◆

Alec's Cell in Nicosia Prison

STELLIOS — You know, yesterday was my birthday.

ALEC — Happy birthday, Stellios.

STELLIOS — Thank you. But it is not so happy. What sort o' kid were you, Alec? You a good kid? You ever steal? It don't matter. I wanted to take my kids to the beach. The oldest boy don't wanna come. He wants the cinema. It's a beautiful day. The sun's shining. I say, 'We're going to the beach!'. You know what he does? He takes a pound from his mother's purse and goes to the cinema. I do what I have to do. I beat him. On my birthday I beat him. The day is closing in tears. My wife, she's looking at me. I say, 'I don't want it this way. He's got to learn. Stealing is wrong.' She says, 'I agree, Stellios, but what is wrong with wanting to go to the cinema?' 'Nothing.' 'So why didn't you let him go?' 'Because I am his father, and it is my birthday and he stole a pound.' 'He stole the pound 'cos you wouldn't let him go to the cinema.' 'So you're saying I was wrong.' 'No! you were right! It's what a father got to do.' 'I don't get it.' Then she says, 'Look, Stellios, for thirty seconds it's absolutely clear what you gotta do. You had to give him a beating. Now you got the rest of the day to think about it.' And she walks away. Where do I stand? You ever feel sorry, Alec?

ALEC — Sorry?

STELLIOS — Yeah. For what you done.

ALEC — Sorry for what happened.

STELLIOS — Yeah. [*Thinking about it*] My wife! She would understand that.

◆ ◆ ◆ ◆ ◆

1983 The Villa in Larnaca

POLICE HAILER (O.S.) — Attention! Attention! Will you accept the approach of First Secretary Dimitri?

KHLOUD — Our home was beautiful. A stone house. Groves of olive and vine. Where the Cypress grew, women in black dresses drew water. Talking about children and marriages, watching their men in the fields, backs stooped to the old way of reaping… I always thought my father was to blame for the catastrophe. Al Nakba! But the Egyptian was wounded and asking for water. We were Christians. A mile up the road was Amwas, where Christ appeared to the disciples. Would you know about that, Alec? The Israelis didn't know what to do with us. Nine thousand without shelter, wandering the roads.

POLICE HAILER (O.S.) — Attention! Attention! Will you accept the approach of First Secretary Dimitri?

KHLOUD — They'll tell you anything. Butros was right, you can't believe what they say. Mother was crying, 'Listen the radio is saying, go back home. They were hardly able to walk. Old people mumbling, flopping down exhausted, some of them had been on the road for days. Babies wailing, children weeping. An Israeli woman soldier gave us a can of water.' 'Why wont they let us go home? Tell them we want our homes back.' My father sat down on the road. He said 'They have no orders, they don't know what to do with us.' For our hunger he rolled grain between his palms to soften, but I let the seed hang in my mouth and spat it to the ground. A soldier picked me up, gave me a sweet. A kind face, but I saw he was weeping. 'My hands are sticky yamma.' His officer shouted 'Clear them out, they are only Arabs. The walk will do them good.'

POLICE HAILER (O.S.) Attention! Attention! Will you accept the approach of First Secretary Dimitri?

KHLOUD We watched from the desolation of the fields as the bulldozers went to work. Our homes became a heap of rubble. The furniture, the rugs, the pigeons and hens, all jumbled up. And my mother's blue dressing gown trapped in the stones. Butros! You see, I have not forgotten the road from Beit Nuba.

ALEC [*Up and training his rifle through the window. Shouts*] Dimitri! Come over! First Secretary? You're a fucking taxi driver!

◆ ◆ ◆ ◆ ◆

1993 Nicosia Prison Visiting Room

ALEC and JAN face each other.

ALEC — Sometimes I feel I have just imagined everything. Ever feel like that?

JAN — There you go again! Talking like a dreamer. In abstracts. Like this was something we dreamed up together. Like debating communism or conscience with your stupid friend Dennis, when you've had a few drinks and you got into one of the stupid arguments, setting the world to rights. You are not in touch with reality! You think you are the only one who ever had to make a decision. There is nothing abstract about putting a gun to somebody's head.

ALEC — Those people they murdered in the camps…

JAN — What?

ALEC — They were real. I know they were real.

JAN — Camps! What camps? Don't steal our history! Don't steal our memories, our feelings…

ALEC — There was something I wanted to tell you…

JAN — [*Recovering herself*] We don't have to go on. We can stop it right here. I'll be honest, this is painful for me.

ALEC — I understand everything you're saying…

JAN — Nothing will alter the way I feel.

ALEC — It isn't about the past. Those long shadows. It's about tomorrow. About something being arranged. My mother will be at the airport. It's about the future.

◆ ◆ ◆ ◆ ◆

1983 The Villa Interior in Larnaca

ALEC is at the window his rifle tracking DIMITRI. KHLOUD enters thrusting DAVID forward. Compelling him to kneel. DAVID is hooded. His hands are tied behind his back with electric flex.

ALEC — Dimitri!

DIMITRI — [*Shouting from outside*] It's finished, Alec! You gotta come out. There's no trade! Sorry, Alec! I tried. I really tried. We're getting the same message from both sides. Disarm and come out! Do yourself a favour, they're not going to wait… The order is to let him go.

ALEC — We need some time. A few minutes…

DIMITRI — Sure! Sure! But do the right thing…

ALEC — What would that be?

DIMITRI — Stay alive! [*DIMITRI leaves*]

KHLOUD — What did you expect? We are always betrayed. It's not so terrible that the leaders betray us. This we accept. But if we betray each other we will fall into darkness. [*Placing the red kaffiyeh scarf around ALEC's neck*] This was my brother's. If I forget him, they will deny what has happened, what they have done, that we ever existed. They will say, 'There is no such thing as a Palestinian.' It is not about revenge. It is about nobody seeing. For such a truth you crossed the world.

[*For a moment it is as if she would wrest the gun from ALEC. ALEC pushes her to one side. Presents the gun to the back of DAVID's head. Fires*]

◆◆◆◆◆

1993 An Office in Nicosia

SINISTER MAN — The last thing we need is to agonise.

JAN — I used to ask myself why I was reassured. A politician saying 'They don't exist – it's not as if they were here first and we pushed them out.' A socialist saying such a thing. Such an absurd thing.

SINISTER MAN — Our friend. Did he express any doubts?

JAN — Who can be one hundred per cent sure of anything?

SINISTER MAN — [*Writing his report*] No doubts! Something to do with being British I suppose. We learnt it from them. It's the colonial thing. Extraordinary people.

JAN — I don't know your name. I've just thought about it. Your name escapes me. Did you tell me and I've forgotten? It doesn't matter.

SINISTER MAN — You've decided against going back? Revulsion, was that? Complete and utter revulsion. Understandable. Cold blooded bastard. The woman... [*Thinks it over*] Reverting to type? [*Reads*] 'Pedigree- anti fascist'. Did you really want to say that?

JAN — Would writing something down, make it true?

SINISTER MAN — [*Reads*] 'And in another space or time might well have come to the rescue of Jews in Europe'. Come on! Come on! This is making problems for yourself...

JAN — [*Over looking the report*] How do you sign your reports? What was it you were telling me about bee-keeping?

SINISTER MAN — [*Concealing the report*] I keep having this nightmare that I'm several different people.

JAN — Is that a good way of avoiding issues?

SINISTER MAN — Being several different people?

JAN — Bee-keeping.

SINISTER MAN — We could talk all night, but they are expecting something. There was no indication of a release date? Nothing by way of a hint?

JAN — How would you put down a reluctance to condemn? How would you explain that? Some kind of consequence of shared guilt? Perhaps? I mean it's the chicken-and-egg thing, isn't it? The whole mess being brought about by the terrorist. In time they are going to see it for themselves.

SINISTER MAN Do you think so?

JAN Well, they just have to ask themselves a simple question. Is the terrorist creating the problem or is the problem creating the terrorist? It's so bloody obvious. You marvel at human credulity.

SINISTER MAN Ah! The mysteries of cause and effect! Hardly original. But it works. [*Returning to the report*] Now! This word 'soldier'. Can't we do something about it? You're a journalist. What would your editor prefer? Alliteration! The implications over and above the logic of speech. I'm sure I don't have to tell you.

JAN But doubtless you will!

SINISTER MAN Strangle! Strife! Strident! Where the tongue hits the roof of the mouth. I always find those sounds… aggressive… positive! I've a boss too, you know. Precise language is what he compliments me on. His father was from Munich. Strike… strafe…

JAN Strawberry!

SINISTER MAN [*Returns to the report*] Soldier… soldier…mm! [*With the sudden delight of inspiration*] Assassin! Much less ambiguous! [*Makes the alteration*] Would you like some coffee?

JAN Basically, you're quite a sociable person.

SINISTER MAN I suppose I am. It's an enormous dilemma.

JAN Can you imagine a way forward that would take no account of revenge?

SINISTER MAN — This has to be faxed in office hours. Say anything you like. The first thing that comes into your head.

JAN — Anything? If Hitler were in a house with twenty innocent people, would it still be necessary to put a bomb there?

SINISTER MAN — Ah! Now, who said that? Don't tell me…

JAN — At the time it seemed unanswerable. What if the twenty innocents were Jews? How would our Mr Shamir have answered?

SINISTER MAN — He would have blown them up. Then he would have said, 'If they were so innocent, what are they doing sharing a house with Hitler?' The fox! You sure you didn't come up with any indication of release? Never any suggestion? I don't want you to feel you are under any pressure.

JAN — Do you feel I am letting you down?

SINISTER MAN — Perhaps. But not to worry. They'll get the bastard anyhow. Even if it takes fifty years. Go to your daughter's wedding. Get on with your life. Let it become someone else's problem.

JAN — I lay awake all night…

SINISTER MAN — Did you? Is there something he told you we don't know about? Or something you are thinking we ought to be considering? It's not important. Nothing is going to change. Just the space at the bottom of a page.

JAN [*JAN walks away. Pauses*] Look! Just write – 'she expressed a doubt.' Will that help? Only put it at the top of the page! [*Exits*]

THE END

The Vicious Circle

Tom Hadaway

This play was first performed by Big Mama Productions in September 1999 on stage at Bede Theatre, The University of Sunderland.

Original Cast

Mary Webb	S.P.O. Janine
Sarah McLane	Bridget McLeod
Val McLane	Mrs Donachie
Jen Brewis	S.P.O. Smith

Directed by Chris Meads and Val McLane

Characters

S.P.O. JANINE	Officer
BRIDGET	Prisoner
MRS DONACHIE	Visitor
P.O.2.	Junior Officer
S.P.O. SMITH	Officer

Abbreviations

P.O.	Prison Officer
S.P.O.	Senior Prison Officer
C.A.C.'s	Central Automatic Control System
G.1 – G.4	Gate One – Gate Four
'H' WING	Cat. A High Security Wing of H.M.P. Durham. (Female)
S.P.V.	Special Purpose Visit
G.O.D.	Governor of Durham

Scene One	1996 Duty Officer's Room 'H' Wing Durham Prison
Scene Two	1997 Visiting Room of 'H' Wing

Scene One

1996 Duty Officer's Room 'H' Wing Durham Prison

Enter BRIDGET followed by S.P.O. SMITH. They sit opposite each other, a table between. S.P.O. SMITH places a tape recorder between herself and BRIDGET.

S.P.O. SMITH [*Switching on recorder*] S.P.O. D. Smith, Day Control, H Wing, HMP Durham. Supervised taped interview on request of Prisoner 7525, Bridget McLeod. Tape Begins… [*Consults watch*] At 10.15 hours in the presence of the aforementioned duty officer, 14th July, 1996. [*To Bridget*] Alright Bridget, your turn, go ahead. Make your statement.

BRIDGET What?

S.P.O. SMITH Say whatever it is you wish Probation to know.

BRIDGET What di ye want us ti say?

S.P.O. SMITH It is not up to me. It is your request Bridget.

BRIDGET What's the fuckin' point?

S.P.O. SMITH Girl! They are bending over backwards to help you. What is it you want them to know? It is up to you! You say you have trouble writing things down. They are giving you this chance to speak out. Now… off you go… In you own words!

BRIDGET How do A start?

S.P.O. SMITH — Your name! Start by saying your name! What is your name?

BRIDGET — Ye know what me fuckin' name is.

S.P.O. SMITH — It is a matter of establishing identity. For the record! State your name.

BRIDGET — Me name is Bridget McLeod... Now What?

S.P.O. SMITH — Your story! Your background! What it is you would like them to learn about you. It is up to you. This is your first week here since your transfer from Styal.

BRIDGET — I want face ti face wi' them.

S.P.O. SMITH — This is as good as face to face. Do yourself a favour Bridget. What is it you want them to know. Keep it clear. Keep it simple. Keep calm. No point in anger. Speak slowly and clearly. They are assessing you! Stick to facts.

BRIDGET — Me name is Bridget McLeod, or Donachie, or somethin' or other... Y' see! I was put into care when I was three an' a half, but always wondered where me mother an' father were an' why they weren't lookin' for me. When I was sixteen I'd give up hope of ever knowing who they were, when this happened. I was working' in a hostel run by nuns in Glasgow. Where old people an' travellers come in for a rest an' a cup o' tea. I got on talkin' with this old lady about where she come from, and I told her about the troubles I'd been in. 'McLeod,' she said, 'Is that ye name?' 'That's right,' I said. 'Bridget McLeod!' 'Would ye know an Annie McLeod?' she said. And I remembered I'd had a sister of that name.

S.P.O. SMITH — And…?

BRIDGET — 'Well love, I'm your grandmother'. the old lady told me. And she directed me to me family who were living on a site near Manchester. And that's how I got back to them.

[*Pause*]

S.P.O. SMITH — Is that it?…

BRIDGET — What it is… I never forgive me mother for not fightin' for me. When she died I was the only one who didn't cry at the funeral. She said, because of what she'd done they had declared her not to be a fit parent, but I felt if she had really loved me she would have fought for me. And now I'm in the same trouble. My two kids are fostered while I am in here and they never write. I don't know if they are gettin' my letters and I don't even know the name an' an address of where they are fostered. My probation officer won't tell me. She says she can't. I don't know what to do. Can you tell me what I should do. I need someone to tell me what to do.

[*Pause*]

S.P.O. SMITH — Alright Bridget! Anything else? Is that your complete statement?

BRIDGET — Request return to cell.

S.P.O. SMITH — End of tape… 10.20 hours. Prisoner 7572 requests return to cell. [*S.P.O. SMITH switches off recorder. Rises and leads BRIDGET off*]

BRIDGET [*Exiting*] I don't want my kids growing up thinking about me the way I thought about my mother.

◆ ◆ ◆ ◆ ◆

Scene Two

1997 Visiting Room of 'H' Wing

Note: This room is at the entrance to the cell block. Visitors are brought in through electronically locked gates, four in number, from the male prison yard. At each gate the visitor is scrutinised by close circuit camera before and after entry. The wing holds thirty six high-risk category female prisoners in an enclave within shouting distance of the thirteen hundred men in the main prison. It is claustrophobic and dubbed 'the submarine' by the inmates. The visiting room is two cells knocked into one (8' x 12'). No one has ever escaped from it since John MacVicar made his spectacular bid in the 1960s when it was a male wing. His escape route, the main ventilation shaft has since been filled with concrete.

S.P.O. JANINE enters. Studies the room furniture, a table and three chairs. Two chairs face across the table. The third is against the wall, slightly elevated, allowing the officer to supervise the interview while remaining aloof. She brings a small vase of flowers for the centre of the table to brighten things up. Satisfied with the set up she sits on the elevated chair to study her clipboard.

INTERCOM (O.S.) [*The entrance buzzer. The crackle of the intercom. The voice of the Wing Controller*] G.1. Open! Cac's on! Cac's on!

[*S.P.O. JANINE alerted. Rises, looks towards the visitor entrance*]

(O.S.)	[*Metallic ring of a gate opening*]
S.P.O. JANINE	[*Speaking into her mobile, which is pinned to her lapel*] G.4… E. and E. clear. [*She looks up at the ceiling*]
(O.S.)	[*A gate closing. Footsteps. Another gate opening*]
MRS DONACHIE	[*MRS DONACHIE enters clutching a plastic carrier bag. Cautious. Overawed. Looks back to thank the unseen escorting officer who has brought her to the gate*] Thank you miss! [*She turns to face S.P.O. JANINE*]
(O.S.)	[*Final ring of the closing gate*]
	[*MRS DONACHIE startled, involuntarily shudders with a feeling of being trapped*]
S.P.O. JANINE	[*Consulting her clip board*] Mrs Donachie?
	[*MRS DONACHIE moves toward the wrong chair*]
	The other chair dear! And head up, look to the camera.
	[*MRS DONACHIE swivels round, unaware of where the camera is*]
	No! Straight ahead. As you were! That's right! Now look up. Right!
INTERCOM (O.S.)	Entrance confirmed and logged. G.4.
S.P.O. JANINE	Empty your bag onto the table.
MRS DONACHIE	[*Looking about the room*] Ye can see how it got the name.

S.P.O. JANINE The contents! On the table… please!

MRS DONACHIE Contents?

S.P.O. JANINE Of the carrier bag.

MRS DONACHIE Oh' wasn't all that done at the Gate Lodge. I tell ye, near up me arse the' was! Be nothin' much left in the way of contents. Sorry' It's the rules! I know, I know! [*Begins fishing into the carrier*] Well named the submarine eh?

S.P.O. JANINE Who calls it that?

MRS DONACHIE It's well known.

S.P.O. JANINE Is it?

MRS DONACHIE 'H' Wing! An' don't the' say it's more secure than a duck's bum. An' that's watertight.

S.P.O. JANINE On the table.

MRS DONACHIE Sorry miss! [*Into the bag, reflecting on what is missing*] Biscuits not allowed! Ciggies not allowed! Scenty soap not allowed! Quality Street! Ah! Jesus, haven't the' took the sweeties!

S.P.O. JANINE Foodstuff! Not allowed. You will get them returned when you leave.

MRS DONACHIE What's left? [*Brings out a jar of pickled beetroot*] They've allowed the pickled beetroot and they's foodstuff.

S.P.O. JANINE That's a mistake.

MRS DONACHIE Then it's their mistake. Not mine!

S.P.O. JANINE — Not allowed!

MRS DONACHIE — Her uncle Sean pickled them beetroot.

S.P.O. JANINE — Did he! [*Confiscating the beetroot*] Glass container! Doubly disallowed! We don't want them cutting up. Do we? What's left?

[*MRS DONACHIE brings out a pullover*]

S.P.O. JANINE — Allowed! Subject to Prisoner Property Ruling! She may already have the statutory two cardigans. Can't have the wing turned into an Oxfam depot, can we? Anything else?

MRS DONACHIE — [*MRS DONACHIE brings out a religious greeting card*] Just this Holy card from Father O'Malley.

S.P.O. JANINE — [*S.P.O. JANINE inspects the card, back and front*] Not allowed!

MRS DONACHIE — Not allowed?

S.P.O. JANINE — No written material allowed until cleared by the Censor's Office. She may get it in due course.

MRS DONACHIE — All it says is 'Blessed Mary let not thy daughter be confounded forever'.

S.P.O. JANINE — Well, there you are then.

MRS DONACHIE — Not readin' somethin' sinister in that are ye?

S.P.O. JANINE — This is Durham Prison Mrs Donachie. Everything, everyone, comes through the Gate shouting 'I'm Innocent.' We have learned to accept nothing at face value.

MRS DONACHIE Father O'Malley is a friend of the Pope!

S.P.O. JANINE Sorry!

MRS DONACHIE He's a very devout priest. And a lovely man!

S.P.O. JANINE I'm sure!

MRS DONACHIE I'll not have him maligned.

S.P.O. JANINE Just be calm Mrs Donachie. You are here on an S.P.V.

MRS DONACHIE Oh, S.P.V. is it? Huh! The jargon. I can't be doin' with it. Makes me head boil.

S.P.O. JANINE S.P.V. Special Purpose Visit. Which is outside of normal visiting. Has been awarded.

MRS DONACHIE Well, there's another fine word. Awarded is it? Think the' was givin' ye somethin' for free.

S.P.O. JANINE Awarded by Governor Graham, who has instructed me to inform you…

MRS DONACHIE 'God' spoke to me!

S.P.O. JANINE Pardon? Who spoke to you?

MRS DONACHIE 'God'! Himself!

S.P.O. JANINE God spoke to you?

MRS DONACHIE He did indeed. Just as I got here.

S.P.O. JANINE How did you know it was God?

MRS DONACHIE — Wasn't He surrounded by all these important people. All of them givin' it the 'Yessir', no sir, three bags full sir!'

S.P.O. JANINE — And what did God say to you?

MRS DONACHIE — He said, 'Good morning Mrs Donachie.'

S.P.O. JANINE — So what did you say?

MRS DONACHIE — I just said 'An' a good mornin' ti you 'God'.' Well, isn't that how ye call him? 'God'! G.O.D. Govenor of Durham. And I'm thinkin' it was the done thing. We was passin' through the Gate Lodge together. He went ti the right! I went ti the left! Seems a very nice fella. And all they men locked up here. A thousand three hundred is it? Comin thro' the yard I see their faces at the windows. And the things they were shoutin'! Disgustin'! I hear they cook the food for these lasses. I hear they piss in it.

S.P.O. JANINE — Mrs Donachie! I understood this was your first ever visit to Durham.

MRS DONACHIE — And so it is.

S.P.O. JANINE — But you are obviously familiar with the prison jargon. 'The Gate Lodge,' 'The Submarine,' 'God'.

MRS DONACHIE — Well, I can explain that. For how it is ye see. Aren't I from the Moss Side? Us Manchester Irish. Haven't we the habit of passin' the talk? Y'understand? Travellin' people! Us muther an' fathers bein' from County Galway. 'Those who have gone before, prepare the way,' is how they'd put it. If ye get the drift.

S.P.O. JANINE — I think I get the drift!

MRS DONACHIE — Well, both experienced ladies are we not? Mind, I'm surprised how young y'are. Poor darlin'. You've a job I'd not want ti take on. A place like this! And you probably doin' as much time as those you've got locked up.

S.P.O. JANINE — And it is my job Mrs Donachie to pass you a message from Mr Graham.

MRS DONACHIE — Ah! 'God' Himself.

S.P.O. JANINE — Governor Graham authorised this S.P.V. following a memo from the Director General... [*Begins to read from file*]

MRS DONACHIE — Director General was it.

S.P.O. JANINE — Director General of Prison Services. In the light of a ruling from the Council of Europe.

MRS DONACHIE — Council of Europe!

S.P.O. JANINE — On the provision of service for the treatment and prevention of mental disorders consequent to long term custodial sentences. While maintaining an integrated regime.

MRS DONACHIE — Integrated regime!

S.P.O. JANINE — So forth and so forth...

MRS DONACHIE — An' so forth!

S.P.O. JANINE — With the need to preserve a prisoner's individuality, humanity and dignity, etc.... I'll go to the final point.

MRS DONACHIE — If ye wouldn't mind…

S.P.O. JANINE — But always bearing in mind the imperative need.

MRS DONACHIE — Imperative need!

S.P.O. JANINE — Of preserving good order and discipline. The officer in charge of this S.P.V. pertaining to prisoner Bridget McLeod… is empowered to terminate this visit at the first sign of trouble.

MRS DONACHIE — Trouble? O' ye'll get no trouble from me. I thank God for the gift of my upbringin!

S.P.O. JANINE — Prisoner 7525, Bridget McLeod is your niece?

MRS DONACHIE — That's right! Second child of me sister Annie… God rest her soul!

S.P.O. JANINE — It is noted here, [*Reads*] Apart from Howard League appointee, there is no recorded visit of friend or close relative of this prisoner in the twelve months since her arrival here in Durham following her transfer from HMP Styal, Cheshire.

MRS DONACHIE — [*Pausing to allow the information to sink in*] And am I to take that as a rebuke. So that I might think shame? Well! I will not think shame.

S.P.O. JANINE — It is a matter of indifference to me Mrs Donachie.

MRS DONACHIE — But I see you writin' tings down.

S.P.O. JANINE — I have a report to make. A job to do, that's all!

MRS DONACHIE — Then write this down. I know well enough no one has been to visit Bridget in the year she has been here. But listen! I was up at four o'clock this mornin', feedin, an, muckin' out the beddin' of animals that cannot be neglected for a day's length. And this before turning, ti the concerns of me own family. How would you know how the likes of us live? And is it only the rich an' famous ye's lock up in this place? Wi' their visitors arrivin' in chauffer driven cars?

S.P.O. JANINE — Mrs Donachie!

MRS DONACHIE — Now you hear me! It's a cold comin' I've had of it. By seven o'clock stood on the by-pass in the pissin' rain waitin' o' the dealer Monaghan ti lift us into central Manchester. An' what time will I be gettin' back? Wi' the last train arrivin' Piccadilly near midnight. What if Monaghan is lyin' somewhere's stoned out his head? What if all the buses has stopped? Get a taxi should A?

S.P.O. JANINE — Mrs Donachie!

MRS DONACHIE — An' where am I ti get taxi money? Flog me mutton ti the taxi driver would ye have me do? For that's how it is for the likes of us. All a matter o' time an' money.

S.P.O. JANINE — Mrs Donachie will you please…

MRS DONACHIE — I'm tellin' the owld fella I'm off ti see our Annie's bairn in Durham, an' he's sayin' 'Where's the money for that comin' from?' And I'm tellin' him, 'No worry on that account for Father O'Malley has put up the cash.' 'Raided the Parish fund has he?' For he's another one sneerin' at the clergy. An' maybe in truth they've things ti answer for.

But when it comes down to helpin' those at the bottom of the ladder. Who speaks for the despised an' rejected? Not your politicians or your pop stars, or your millionaires or ye mayors of the City. Only the likes o' Father O'Malley. Besides! Wasn't he me last hope of a few bob!

S.P.O. JANINE — Mrs Donachie…

MRS DONACHIE — You's think we're rubbish! An' your prison here is the rubbish bin.

S.P.O. JANINE — This is not my prison.

MRS DONACHIE — Who's is it then? For it's not mine.

S.P.O. JANINE — You know why Bridget is here!

MRS DONACHIE — I do! It's ti make the numbers up. Sure it is. For this is no place for the likes of her.

S.P.O. JANINE — You know that being here is of her own making.

MRS DONACHIE — A birra hoist! A birra blaggin! Tryin' ti feed her bairns.

S.P.O. JANINE — She was transferred here from…

MRS DONACHIE — From the other side of Britain. Hundreds o' miles from her background. Outa sight! Outa mind! All that matters!

S.P.O. JANINE — Brought here! Following determined escape bids. First, from the Remand Centre of Risley.

MRS DONACHIE — Huh' Grisley Risley!

S.P.O. JANINE — And then from HMP Styal. Where she scaled the outer perimeter…

MRS DONACHIE — And so she did! An' I'll tell ye about that. For didn't we all hear about it on the site. The reason she legged it out o' there was on account o' they builders repairin' the fence. Weren't they leavin' scaffoldin' an' planks an' stuff. Ye've ti understand Bridget is a sunshine girl. Used ti the open air an' starry skies. Ti the wild grass an' moorland spaces. If a girl like that sees a ladder, isn't it a stairway ti the stars? Ye'd have ti blame they builders miss. Unless, ye lay it at the door of the Prisoner Rehabilitation Officers. Tellin' poor girls ti rise about their criminal dependency. To being usin' their own initiative and express themselves through activity. Well, she done just that didn't she?

S.P.O. JANINE — Your niece now has an extended sentence. With the loss of all remission and privileges. So Mrs Donachie! Three and a half years to go with no prospect of parole.

MRS DONACHIE — Why you tellin' me this? What is the point? Givin' me the third degrees are ye? I'm just here on a S.P.V. aren't I? Has somethin' happened? Somethin's happened! What's happened? Bridget shouldn't even be in a place like this. With all they monsters! You know that!

S.P.O. JANINE — The policy of sentence is nothing to do with us. That is for the Courts and the Judges Mrs Donachie. As Prison Officers we cope with the aftermath, the problems of custody.

MRS DONACHIE — And who is in here with her? Tell me that! Behind that wall! You know who's here. That one's here isn't she!

S.P.O. JANINE — Who are you talking about?

MRS DONACHIE — You know who I'm talking about.

S.P.O. JANINE — How can I unless you tell me.

MRS DONACHIE — You know who I mean! *Her!*

S.P.O. JANINE — Who?

MRS DONACHIE — *She's* here isn't she! *Her!* Ugh! Cannot bring myself ti say her name. But you know.

S.P.O. JANINE — Mrs Donachie! Home Office regulations forbid our discussing or revealing the identity of inmates. So you may as well…

MRS DONACHIE — You know! *Her!* That monster! That beast! That cursed thing! [*She makes the sign of the cross*] That Hindley! And is this where that loony Lord Longford comes lustin! For that… that… I cannot say woman, for she can't be a woman… That limb o' Satan. Oh' my God, on the other side o' that wall is she? Sends a shiver thro' ye.

S.P.O. JANINE — You have been warned Mrs Donachie.

MRS DONACHIE — A creature like that! Torturin' an morderin' helpless children.

S.P.O. JANINE — Any trouble and I am to terminate this visit.

MRS DONACHIE — Under the same roof and alongside a young muther who is only here because she wanted to feed hers.

S.P.O. JANINE [*Using her mobile. Inserting her ear plug*] Control One! S.P.O. to G.O.D.

MRS DONACHIE What in God's name were the' thinkin' of?

S.P.O. JANINE Hello G.O.D. It is sir! Yes sir! No sir! I see! I will sir! Yes sir! Of course sir! Yes sir! No sir!

MRS DONACHIE [*Aside*] T'ree bags full sir!

S.P.O. JANINE [*Closing down mobile. Removing ear piece*] Mrs Donachie, I am instructed to proceed, but the caution to terminate still applies.

MRS DONACHIE Himself was that?

S.P.O. JANINE However I have to inform you that this interview is now being cassette videod.

MRS DONACHIE Oh' It's on the tele are we? [*Looks around*]

S.P.O. JANINE For internal use only.

MRS DONACHIE Fly on the wall is there?

S.P.O. JANINE For in house, officer training purpose. But you are entitled to be made aware.

[*MRS DONACHIE fusses her hair*]

Bridget is at the point of entry. Post medication! And is aware of your being here.

MRS DONACHIE Post medication! An' what's that when it's at home? Pumpin' her full o' drugs are ye?

S.P.O. JANINE We are trying to do what is best for everyone!

MRS DONACHIE — Somethin's happened you aren't tellin' me…

S.P.O. JANINE — Governor Graham is instituting a liberalising approach. He is hoping you might help us to implement new Home Office guidelines.

MRS DONACHIE — Me! Help you's!

S.P.O. JANINE — In everyone's interest. Including Bridget.

MRS DONACHIE — Wasn't me put her in here.

S.P.O. JANINE — Nor did we! I must repeat, Mrs Donachie, Prison Officers are not the judiciary. We are only here to keep the lid on. Whether we agree with Bridget being here in this High Security unit, or approve of who she is banged up with, is of no relevance. She is here, full stop! End of story! Except that it isn't.

MRS DONACHIE — You gonna tell me what's happened? Being fightin' has she? Laid one on a screw did she? Oh' I shouldn't call ye that. Screws! Ye don't like that. I'm sorry! And I know the temper the girl has. Wilful it is! And was it yourself got thumpted?

S.P.O. JANINE — There was an altercation Mrs Donachie. Subject now of an internal inquiry, and yes, Bridget was involved.

MRS DONACHIE — I thought so!

S.P.O. JANINE — Bridget is not on report. There will be no punishment. And it may not be discussed in the present context.

MRS DONACHIE — Ah! Ye'll have ye hands full wi' that one!

S.P.O. JANINE — Hear me out Mrs Donachie! [*Demonstrating document*] The Prison Psychiatric Service recognise women are probably more resilient in coping with long term sentence, but appreciate they have more to lose and suffer greater stress.

It is pointed out here [*Reads*] A man may do two-three years, come out, meet up with a pal, go for a pint, and resume his life. Start again where he left off. A woman on the other hand may well feel her life is ruined and reconnecting beyond her power. She is more likely to have suffered the loss of all that was central to her existence. Her home, her family, her house, furniture…

MRS DONACHIE — Furniture! That's a laugh! Not two sticks ti rub tigether!

S.P.O. JANINE — …her reputation, her friends.

MRS DONACHIE — Better off wi' the loss. For the kind o' friends she kept the company of.

S.P.O. JANINE — …her children.

MRS DONACHIE — Now ye at the point! Tell her where they're kept.

S.P.O. JANINE — That is the business of the Probationary Service.

MRS DONACHIE — That's passin' the buck!

S.P.O. JANINE — We don't make the rules.

MRS DONACHIE — She'll be out o' her mind about those two kids. But as ye say, what is it ti you?

S.P.O. JANINE — What it is to us Mrs Donachie? Is precisely this! We have to live with these stressed individuals. You may, or may not arrive here for an occasional visit, but we are stuck here day and night. Month after month, year to year! And when they crack… we have to cope. I can tell you it is not easy. On top of this job, I also have a family! Do you understand?

MRS DONACHIE — Steady on! Don' forget the candid camera!

S.P.O. JANINE — The public think they've gottem safe behind bars, end of problem! They have no idea.

MRS DONACHIE — Well, it's what ye well paid for is it not? An' maybe ye owld Jack Straw is comin' up wi' the answer. For isn't he of the mind ti lock'm away at ten years of age. I suppose he'd just have'm put in wi' their mams. 'New Labour keeps the family tigether.'

S.P.O. JANINE — There's not much time Mrs Donachie. Perhaps you might like to tell me something about Bridget. About her background.

MRS DONACHIE — Ye probably know more than me!

S.P.O. JANINE — We know she was put into care very young.

MRS DONACHIE — Very young! Three an' a half she was! That young enough for ye's? We never knew her as a child. First I ever see of her, was this red cheeked, raw boned young lassie humpin' down off the back of a fish wagon. Was the one ran overnight from Glasgow ti

Fleetwood. Green tam o' shanter tugged over her lugs an' her hair hung about her shoulders like frozen string. O' rough an' bowld she was, wi' her big loud voice. 'Which o' yous is McLeod?'

An' there was me sister, poor injured soul! How many years she'd sat in that corner, wi' tears streamin' down her face, an' us sayin' 'leave her be. She's thinking about Bridget'. An' suddenly here was her child.

'Which o' yous is McLeod?'

'I'm a McLeod,' says Annie.

'Then I'm thinkin' I'm ye daughter,' says Bridget. 'An if I'm not, I'll just have ti go on bein' nobody's.'

What a homecomin'!

But like all that's new in a house she was made a fuss of. We all did us best. Kat'leen give her a sofa. Alice come up wi' curtains an' blinds, an' most everyone chucked in wirra pot or a pan. But she was never grateful, Not her! Always at a distance. Hard as the hobs. Even when Annie died, God rest her, not a tear. For the muther that had wept buckets for her. Could never work the girl out. She was no longer one of us. I think I've worked it out now! For I see her in the same trouble.

S.P.O. JANINE — She has to have somewhere to return. Somewhere she belongs.

MRS DONACHIE — An' what di ye expect from me?

S.P.O. JANINE — You can remind her of those she knew. You can tell her there is a future.

MRS DONACHIE — Promise her a lie!

S.P.O. JANINE — If you have to.

MRS DONACHIE — Her only future is her past! Waitin' for it's come back.

(O.S.) — [*Intercom buzzer*]

[*S.P.O. JANINE rises, moves to entrance*]

(O.S.) — [*Gate opening/closing*]

[*BRIDGET enters escorted by P.O.2. She is clutching a flask and two cups. Keeps her gaze down and is led to her chair. Sits. Stares at the flowers and empty carrier bag on the table. S.P.O. JANINE returns to her seat. P.O.2 Takes up a standing position alongside. S.P.O. JANINE signals Mrs Donachie to engage her niece. The two officers affect disconcern, putting their heads together over the clipboard*]

MRS DONACHIE — Bridget!

[*BRIDGET looks up at Mrs Donachie, seeming not to recognise her*]

How are ye darlin'? Good ti see ye again.

[*From BRIDGET comes a thin smile of recognition/pleasure*]

That's it girl! A wee smile.

S.P.O. JANINE — You know who this is Bridget?

MRS DONACHIE — Sure she does! Your Aunty Cait! Aren't 'I? The one does all the 'talking' Ye'd not ever forget me.

[*BRIDGET'S smile broadens*]

S.P.O. JANINE — Cups an' flask on the table Bridget! Bridget has brought you a coffee Mrs Donachie.

MRS DONACHIE — Coffee! Isn' that lovely. Just what the doctor ordered. Didn't think the owld Durham nick provided such a service! Oh' I could settle down here. [*To the P.O.s*] Is this cos we's on the tele?

[*The P.O.'s reaction shows Mrs Donachie has scored a point. Bridget puts the cups on the table. Attempts to pour the flask. Fumbles. Fails. Gives up*]

MRS DONACHIE — There! Take your time luv. Here, let me help! [*MRS DONACHIE reaches toward Bridget*]

S.P.O. JANINE — Let her manage. She can manage.

[*BRIDGET unsteadily beings to pour. Half fills the cups*]

MRS DONACHIE — [*Withdrawing her arm*] Everyone sends their love. Padraig! Kat'leen! Annie! Donal! Tomas! An' Father O'Malley! He hopes ye keepin' ti yor faith. Not a day passes but he intercedes ti the Sacred Heart. An' I am ti remind ye that God prefers prayers ti tears.

[*BRIDGET sits, distracted by the empty carrier bag*]

Uncle Sean sent ye some of his pickled beetroots. But I think these here is worried ye might spill'm on the white linen. Michael is away ti America. Well, hasn't he been watchin' an' waitin' his chance ti be off. Like ye own da! Cursin' those he grew up wi' an' thinkin' the leavin' of them would change his luck. Owld Padriag still talks to his pigeons. Dorty, shitty things. An' still smokes that dreadful pipe. He's ownly two teeth left in his bottom jaw, so hasn't he the devil's job ti keep it in his mouth. Took the lend of her top set from his poor missus.

'Are wi havin' a meal?' she says.

'No', just borrowin' them ti grip me pipe,' he says. 'Ye can have'm back for the supper.'

Y'see, nothin' changes! Wi might all get back ti Blackpool later in the year, but it's getting' harder for Travellers ti find a welcome.

[*BRIDGET transfers her attention to the flowers. Touching them*]

MRS DONACHIE Aren't they pretty? Y'mam grew a flower like them. Y'remember? I think these'd do better in a basket an' outa doors. Doesn't all flowers need the wash o' sunlight. How sad an' pale ye look. What disturbs ye me love? This is a strict place is it not, stricter than the other prisons ye've been. Oh dear, so many prisons. How di ye spend the days? Have ye begun ti think more kindly of ye mam? Hadn't she the touch wi' the flowers? When she died Bridget, the darkness of the world fell on us. She loved ye Bridget. Ye mam loved ye. With all her heart an' soul. An' wi' all that great helpless longin' that laid waste to her. Ye know that now don't ye?

BRIDGET My children! Where are my children?

MRS DONACHIE [*Turning to S.P.O. JANINE*] Why is she like this? I never see her like this. [*Turning to Bridget*] I know it must be so hard for ye dear. All these locked doors.

BRIDGET Rosie an' Eleen! Aunty Cait, I need ti know where they are.

MRS DONACHIE But there's more hope in a door that's locked than the grave.

BRIDGET They never write. I don't know if they are gettin' my letters.

MRS DONACHIE Ye poor mam. She was so lonely after ye!

BRIDGET They won't tell me where they are. [*BRIDGET transfers her attention to the flowers. Touching them*]

MRS DONACHIE [*MRS DONACHIE reaches across the table and takes hold of Bridget's hand*] Let them find no fault with ye Bridget. They's not bad people. Its just they don' know what ti do.

BRIDGET Won't tell me!

MRS DONACHIE I know Bridget! They has their own reasons for everythin'. They's not our reasons. But they are tryin' their best. [*Referring to S.P.O. JANINE*] This lady is a muther. She understands. It's not that difficult ti understand.

BRIDGET Why won't they tell me?

MRS DONACHIE Don't cause trouble darlin! They don't want more trouble! This place is full of trouble! Isn't there all sorts in here. There's refugees, there's poor people, sick people, addicts, mental handicapped. The homeless! Some is snarlin' like beasts. Some is cryin's like babies. Some innocent, some guilty, victims, an' monsters. All on the bottom. All lumped tigether. An' here is ye poor self.

But don't the' say, everyone gets a second chance. Isn't that what the' say? [*Cynically*] An' when the' do, owld Ireland will be free, an' there'll be free Christmas puddin's for all the Travellin' folk. Oh' I shouldn't joke. It's a serious thing for ye. Darlin' wi' mus' do what pleases them as has the keys! If only wi could draw a line on the past, we would stop the dead playin' jokes on wi'. But remember God is between us an' all harm.

[*On impulse S.P.O. JANINE hands back the holy card to Mrs Donachie who hands it on in turn to Bridget. BRIDGET reads the card. But drops it listlessly onto the table. MRS DONACHIE retrieves it. Rises. Goes round the table to press it again on Bridget. Lifts Bridget from her chair. Locks her in an embrace. S.P.O. JANINE and her fellow officer are alarmed that it may be getting out of hand but JANINE restrains P.O.2. from interfering. MRS DONACHIE'S head is between Bridget and the officers*]

MRS DONACHIE Take it! Read it! Father O'Malley is sendin' ye the love o' Christ. Hold it ti ye heart. Bridget! Mary muther o' God 'Let not Thy daughter be confounded forever'.

BRIDGET [*Confidentially to her aunt's ear*] Her blood was everywhere! Over the landin'. Down the steps! A shouted 'Y'bastard! Ye evil bastard!' An' A pushed her. Before she hit the bottom A was down kickin' the shit out of her. Kickin' an Kickin'... An' they was all screamin' 'Beast! Beast! Kick the Beast! Kick the Beast!'

S.P.O. JANINE — That's enough. [*To P.O.2*] Separate them! Get her back to the flat.

[*P.O.2. moves in to wrestle the two women apart. Tenaciously they cling together*]

MRS DONACHIE — Who? Who was it?

BRIDGET — Wasn't even born when she done her crime. She was in this prison before I was born.

MRS DONACHIE — Who? Who ye talkin' about?

S.P.O. JANINE — [*Into mobile*] Access G.4 McLeod returning.

BRIDGET — I'm sorry. I'm sorry.

S.P.O. JANINE — Request nursing sister.

BRIDGET — I shouldn't have done it. What was she to do with me.

S.P.O. JANINE — S.P.V. suspended! Over! [*Switches off mobile*]

MRS DONACHIE — Who? Who was to do with ye?

BRIDGET — Myra!

MRS DONACHIE — Myra?

BRIDGET — She wanted ti be friends. I can be ye friend she said.

MRS DONACHIE — Oh my God. That's vile.

BRIDGET — So I pushed her down the steps.

MRS DONACHIE Then ye done right. Thee've nowt ti be sorry for.

P.O.2 Right! Break it up. Come on!

(O.S.) *Steel gates opening left and right.*

S.P.O. JANINE Don't be stupid Bridget. Don't end up on report.

BRIDGET I'm sorry.

MRS DONACHIE Be proud Bridget. What ye done. Ye done for us all.

BRIDGET It done no good.

P.O.2 Come on! Come on!

S.P.O. JANINE Let go Bridget! Just making things worse.

MRS DONACHIE Ye done it for all our children everywhere! God bless ye Bridget.

BRIDGET What about my children? What's it done for them? A was kickin' me own… Aunty Cait! A was kickin' me own kids.

S.P.O. JANINE Let go of her Mrs Donachie.

MRS DONACHIE Ye was doin' God's will.

CONTROL (O.S.) What the fuck is goin' on?

BRIDGET I'll give her the holy card.

MRS DONACHIE You will not. Never!

BRIDGET That's what I'll do.

MRS DONACHIE No' Not ti that beast. [*They grapple for the card*] Think of Father O'Malley.

BRIDGET I'll tell her I'm sorry.

CONTROL (O.S.) To the gate now!

MRS DONACHIE Ye'll do nothing' of the kind.

BRIDGET Then tell me what to do. My kids, they's growin' up thinkin' about me the way I thought about my muther. I don't want that.

[*P.O.2. separates the two women and hustles BRIDGET off*]

Please. Tell me what ti do. Please Aunty Cait! Please! Somebody! [*Exits*]

(O.S.) *The clang of a gate closing.*

[*MRS DONACHIE and S.P.O. JANINE stand and allow themselves time to recover*]

S.P.O. JANINE You alright? Mrs Donachie! Steady! Take your time. I'll escort you to the gate lodge. Mrs Donachie?

[*MRS DONACHIE has won possession of the holy card and doesn't quite know what to do with it*]

Just leave that on the table. I'll look after it.

MRS DONACHIE What will happen to her?

S.P.O. JANINE They will give her something to make her sleep… Come along Mrs Donachie. [*Into Mobile*] S.P.O. Janine Smith terminating S.P.V. prisoner 7525 and visitor Mrs Donachie. Time: thirteen zero six. Escorting

Mrs Donachie and proceeding to gate lodge.

CONTROL (O.S.) Well done Janine!

[MRS DONACHIE closes to S.P.O. Janine at the exit]

S.P.O. JANINE Look up to the camera Mrs Donachie and then do the same when we pass to the other side.

[MRS DONACHIE raises her head to the camera, addressing it directly]

MRS DONACHIE Excuse me! If ye don't mind me sayin'! Isn't this all a bit of a mess? You up there. The one the' call 'God'. Don't ye tink ye should be gettin' ye'sel' down here an' sortin' tings out? I mean we're just people an' we don't know what ti do for the best. Listen! I'm speakin' now for the children. Sure, us was wilful! Sure, us made the mess in the first place. But we was yesterday's children, an' what I'm sayin' is, 'What about tomorrow's children?' Ye cannot let it go on an' on like this. Think of those not yet born. Ye can't just sit there bein' omnipotent! Watchin' us thro' a hole in the roof.

[S.P.O. JANINE has stepped ahead of Mrs Donachie out of the range. of the camera and is regarding her with a mix of apprehension and approval]

For God's sake, 'God'! This could seriously undermine yer authority! Get yoursel' down here, an' get it sorted!

[S.P.O. JANINE gives a thumbs up sign. An approving smile. They exit together. Voices receding]

S.P.O. JANINE (O.S.) Might meet up with him at the gate lodge.

MRS DONACHIE (O.S.) Give'm anuther piece o' me mind.

S.P.O. JANINE (O.S.) Look up at the camera again Mrs Donachie. That's right! That's right! Never got your coffee! Prison Visitor Aid Society! They help with fares. You should call in the office.

MRS DONACHIE (O.S.) Janine! That what the' call ye? Janine! That's a lovely name. Sure it is!

(O.S.) *Decisive clang of a steel gate closing.*

CONTROL (O.S.) G.1 Exit confirmed and logged.

THE END

Postcard from God

Tom Hadaway

This play was first performed in 2001 by The Live Theatre Company as part of a series of Mystery Plays.

Original Cast

Judy Earl Judy

Directed by Max Roberts

Characters

JUDY

Postcard from God

Judy has spent eighteen years a prisoner in H.M.P., sixteen spent on Durham 'H' Wing. Eventually released on evidence which proved her innocence. She has received an invitation from G.O.D. (Governor of Durham) to speak before the Criminal Cases Review Commission[1] *as an example of a miscarriage of justice.*

Now in her early forties, she was a young girl of twenty-three when first imprisoned.

Staying with her mam, Judy wonders how to respond.

A kitchen: a chair; a table; a teapot; a packet of Kelloggs All-Bran.

JUDY enters. Studying a postcard. Taking up a pen and writing pad. Reading what she has set down.

JUDY Dear G.O.D.,

Ya postcard was lovely. But I write this from me mam's where I presently am at! An her on at us ti get in touch. Bein' a right one fer the good manners. She says, 'Not everyday a girl is gettin' a postcard from 'God'. Always naggin'. Right now aren't I sat waitin' of her bell ti ring. Then I'll be takin' up her pot o' tea an' her All-Bran. There's piety fer ya! Kelloggs All-Bran! There's devotion! There's withered owld taste buds! 'I do hate the bloody stuff,' she says. 'Then why eat it?' I says, 'with no sugar.' 'Cos' I'm grateful the way it is', she says. 'It's fer me own good. Ya build up ya store in heaven by ya sufferin below. There is no other way.' Doesn't mean we have ti be grateful does it?

---

[1] Criminal Cases Review Commission Created in 1996 to examine and review alleged miscarriages of justice. An independent body, unfunded, and without power to over rule court decisions, merely to decide whether an applicant has a possible chance of success given a further hearing.

JUDY (Cont) 'Ah', she says, 'If it leaves ya bum the same shape an' colour it entered ya gob, it's a sure sign no harm's been done.' Then she says, 'The Kelloggs packaging is ninety per cent made from recycled material. It says so on the box.' So she's doin' her bit fer the environment. I'd say the feckin' contents is ninety per cent recycled material. But what is the point arguin'?

I did in fact get up ti Durham town on the day ya suggested. An' sunny it was, like on ya picture postcard.

[*Light up: Panoramic view of Durham City from below the south-bound platform of the station*]

There it lay below us. Built on its green hills. Ya other Jerusalem. Holdin' out its bright arms. Castle! Bridges! Parks! Markets! With all ya Geordie folk goin' about their lives. An' above it all that great Cathedral. Crownin' the set! Ya Eternal City 'God'! Before me eyes. For a while wasn't I in ya raptures! Then wasn't I rememberin' ya poet. How did he describe it?

Half Church of God, half Castle 'gainst the Scot.[2]

Too bloody true, A thought. There's more ti that architecture than salvation.

Thus did Hope deceive me as she deceiveth All.

Thank ya, Sir Walter Thingy? How well ya read the stones. Didn't I just get back on the train ti rainy feckin' Manchester.

[*JUDY stops reading to speak directly to G.O.D.*]

Sorry! I knew ye'd be waitin' with those important people in the County Hotel. Criminal Cases Review Commission? Never heard o' them! Who are the'? Last resort of the wrongfully convicted? Or the latest resort of them sufferin' delusions of innocence? So, what would A be sayin' ti them? 'Di ya still remember me? The celebrity prisoner stood on the steps of the Old

---

[2] Scott, W., Harold the Dauntless, 1817.

JUDY (Cont) Bailey. Free at last. Triumphantly punchin' the air?' Are the' really still tryin' ti put the system right? [*Pausing*] I'm rememberin' the first time we met. Me on us hands an' knees. Endlessly scrubbin' an' moppin' the walkway into the block. An' fer no other reason but that it stopped us thinkin'. It were the first time I become aware of ya 'God'! You arrivin' new to the place. Ya feet was level with me head. Sayin', 'Sorry for steppin' on ya floor prisoner.' An' me snappin' back wi' all the frustration an' filth pourin' from us. 'It's no ma feckin' floor. It's yor feckin' floor. An' ya can have it feckin' back, soon as ye feckin' like.' Then ya calm, reasonin' voice. 'Officer! This floor was bein' scrubbed at eight thirty this morning. It is now twelve thirty. Why is it still being scrubbed?'

'The prisoner refuses to operate her sewing machine sir.'

'I beg your pardon?'

'Contravention of rule seventeen sir.'

'But regardless of rule seventeen officer, the floor remains and is spotless.'

An' I lifted me head above the level of ya boots and us eyes met. Somethin' flashed between us. It were me Mary Magdalene moment. This 'God's' a decent fella! This 'God's' on us side. This 'God's' doin' his best. An' it was then A fell for ya! I swear ya head was shinin'. Radiant! 'Course ya was twenty year younger then. An let's face it. We weren't exactly spoiled fer choice. Closest I'd been to a good lookin' fella in two year. But it was ya belief in innocence! That's what won me.

Now ye'll be thinkin' I've letcha down. But whose innocence was it 'God'? Yours or mine? Seein' that great cathedral the other day. Us heart failed us 'God'! Ya don't mind us still callin' ye that? In the familiar way of an owld con. As Governor of Durham, signin' yesel' G dot O dot D dot 'God' ya was ti me. [*She consults the postcard*] Now aren't I lookin' fer that other place of yours? Quarried from the same stone. With the same

JUDY (Cont) architectural belief. The one as walls ya evil in, like Cuthberts walls it out. I mean ya Nick! Where! as a young lass of twenty five weren't I holed up fer the crime I never commit. The IRA bomber that never was. 'Til all my young days were gone an' I were handed down ti middle age. Talk about outa sight, outa mind. Not even on ya picture postcard. But look at Cuthbert's pile. All high an' mighty! stood like forever!

How come I live in that city sixteen year, an' this is the first time I ever clap eyes on that monumental heap? 'Course it were three in the mornin' when the' first brung me an' didn't I leave in an armoured van wit blacked out windas? Comin' an' goin' in the dark. Like birth! Like death! An' all my longin' for the family of me own, that brown-haired Irish lad and the green fields of Monaghan, all lost forever! Would this be what ya wanted me sayin'? To ya Criminal Cases Review Commission? Somethin' about redemption? Or maybe forgiveness? But I tell a lie. I did glimpse it once. In the first two year wasn't I on the suicidal mode? Cuttin' up wouldn't cha guess! Pair o' feckin' scissors left careless in the workshop. They'd rushed me ti the dispensary. Top floor o' the wing. An' outa this little winda just beyond the bars, I see the tower! The sun were settin' behind it. An' the sky were full o' red an' gold, wit bits o' purple. An' I stood rooted ti the spot. Tears were formin' in me eyes. So I wept! For who or for why I have no idea, but I think I were realisin' everyone needs a reason for carryin' on livin' even in the depths of despair. Always the first two year before ya long term con understands the pain of what is layin' ahead.

> And Sleep will not lie down, but walks Wild-eyed and cries to Time.[3]

An' thank you 'God' givin' me first sight of that dear poet who spoke for us all. 'Til ya Chief Officer Mrs Hardwick reared up! Remember her? The Anvil of the

---

[3] Wilde, O., *The Ballad of Reading Gaol,* 1898.

JUDY (Cont) North! Durham's answer to Saddam Hussein. The Scud missile!

Me pad? Nine foot by five foot an' that might be an exaggeration. Ya Cath'lic Chaplain give us this book an Cuthbert's tomb were the same dimension. Nine foot by five foot! But at least he were dead when his monks chucked him in. Wasn't us buried alive in the same space? An' I were innocent. Sixteen year later, a Lord Chief Justice said so. Innocent! Like Paddy Hill an' Giuseppe Conlon. Like ya Guildford Four. Ya Birmingham Six. Ya Maguire Seven.

The whole system, he said, 'Littered with people innocent of the crimes for which they have been convicted.' Is this what the' want ti hear? This Criminal Cases Review Commission? 'Is it Irish ya were? Or ya muther, or ya da were it? Are ya Jewish or Palestinian? Catholic or Kosovan? Serbian or gipsy? Or are ya just one o' them feckless feckin' poor. Wonderin' which way ti turn.'

Am I doin' them a disservice? Not ya do-gooders again is it? Had us fill o' them. 'God'! Remember the time ya was windin' us up? With that wife from The Prayers for the Prisoners Committee?

'Would you be Judy?'

'I am.' As if she didn't know. Nosey owld bag!

'And what ye doin' on this High Security wing dear?

As if she give a shite.

'Ye don't mind us askin'?'

'Not at all.'

But you 'G.od' were whisperin' in me lug. 'Tell her it was for shop liftin'.'

'Shop liftin'?' she says.

'Yeh!' I says, 'Shop liftin'.'

'But this is 'H' wing.'
'That's right.'

JUDY (Cont) 'And they have you marked Category 'A'.'

'That's right. Twenty five years I got…'

'For shop lifting?'

'That's right.'

'So they've put you here among all these terrible offenders. Terrorists! Murderers! Bombers!'

'Right!'

'How awful for you…'

'Too true. And things rubs off.'

'Bombers?'

'Shop lifters.'

'Really!'

'But ye see I did a gud job.'

'Shop lifting?'

'That's right! Didn't I lift 'em from one street ti the next.'

Didn't her face now take on the aspect of the donkey's arse! 'I don't think that is funny young lady.'

Neither did I. Five year later weren't that owld cow on the panel for us hoped for transfer ti the pastures green of Cookham Wood, where I might have looked again with …wistful eye

> Upon that little tent of blue
> Which prisoners call the sky.[4]

But that were me. Own worst enemy. With a little help from yesel'. Though give ya due! Ya warned us. Watch out for them do-gooders. Short on the laughs they are. Then maybe there is things we can't be laughin' at.
That north-east writer you were always singin' the praise of? Jewish fella! Planned a comedy about

[4] Wilde, O., ibid.

JUDY (Cont) Auschwitz. Bloody hell! What's funny about a concentration camp?

'Evil' he said, 'Is ya ultimate in Absurdity.' 'Ya Hitler, Eichmann, Goering! Look at their faces. Mad as feckin' hatters.' Believed in Prisons. More prisons. Bigger prisons. Prisons for the sick. Prisons for the old. Prisons for the young. Prisons for the handicapped. Prisons for the refugees. They are all alike, with this pathetic faith in prisons. Ya Michael Howard, ya Jack Straw! Look at their faces. Like barbed wire! Mock them! Cecil Taylor! That were him! Genius!

[*O.S. The bell rings. JUDY glances off. Pause*]

Criminal Cases Review Commission? So would ya have us make'm smile? Could tell'm about the teddy bears and poor owld Ruth. Five year on the soft toy workshop, when her parole application failed. So she come ti me! 'Help me Judy! I'm crackin' up. Stitichin' they feckin' feet on they feckin' teddy bears. Week in, week out. I've another five year ti go. I can't take any more. Tell us what ti do Judy!' 'I'll have a word wit 'God', I said. 'He's got the answers.' An' you 'God', whispered in me ear once again. 'Tell her, sew the feckin feet on back ti front. Not every teddy. Just at random. Every third or fifth. So they don't know whether they're comin' or goin'.'

An' you meant the screws, not the teddies. Come back in Mrs Hardwick! 'Alreet Hinny! Dispensary time! Where's the liquid cosh.'

[*O.S. The bell rings.*]

[*JUDY calls off*] Alright Mam! Just sortin' out 'God's' purpose. All-Bran is comin'.

[*She turns again to G.O.D.*] But what of the too long confined? Who only you may forgive! Who go

JUDY (Cont) …silently round and round,…
[While] through each hollow mind
The memory of dreadful things
Rushe[s] like a dreadful wind,
An horror stalked before each man,
And terror creep[s] behind.[5]

'God'! Y'remember me mam's first visit ti Durham. Two hundred mile she'd travelled, an' we was in the visitin' room feelin' somethin' important had ti be said. Somethin' meaningful!

'But A'm innocent mam!'

'I know that love. Try an' stay calm.'

Then suddenly she came out with it.

'Is she here?'

'Who?'

'*Her.*'

'Who ya talkin' about muther?'

'You know who A'm talkin' about.'

'How can A if ya don' say?'

'You know who A mean.'

'Who?'

'Cannit bring mesel' ti say her name.'

'Then how di ye expect me ti know?'

'That spawn o' satan.'

And I guessed. An' wasn't she in the visitin', Lord Longford just havin' left.

I called over. 'Hi! Myra. This is me mam.'

---

[5] Wilde, O., ibid.

JUDY (Cont) Didn't me mam near have a fit.

'Judy, ya mustn't talk ti people like that.'

'Muther! There is no one else here. Only people like that. Us is all tigether under the one roof.'

But everyone has ti draw a line somewhere. In hatred or love! Now, I see all their faces. Those wi' burdens too deep fer tears. Lined with pain. With regret. The hope drained out o' them. And those hapless sods who were there just ti make the numbers up. Shufflin' round. Charged with terrible bewilderment. You tell me, Mr. Cecil Taylor, what's funny about someone so desperate they try to end their life?

Tell 'm about Mary! Oh yeh! Mary! She was ill. A mean really ill. No-one takin' a blind bit o' notice. Got no sympathy from us A can tell ya. What di ya expect? Us had us bird ti do. Stone me! I had twenty, maybe thirty year ti get thro' without copin' with dreadfully sick people. There she went on… 'I'm gonna kill mesel!' I'm gonna kill mesel'. I'm talkin' about every night y'know, when we was all tryin' ti get some sleep. Well the' had her drugged up all day. That would be when ya Mrs Hardwick wanted some sleep. They were pumpin' Mary full o' drugs. But she was comin' out o' them at night when the rest of us were turnin' in.

'I wanna die! I Wanna die!'

In the strips ya know! A smock. A mattress on the floor. No way she could harm herself.

'If ye don't let us outa here I'm countin' ti ten, then I'm gonna kill mesel.'

Night after night. Fer Chris' sake let her get on with it. Count ti ten?

Didn't we all shout back. Ten, nine, eight, seven, six. Didn't wi try ti help her! Help her top herself. If we could! We would! But then, didn't she get this idea hersel'. She's lookin' at the alarm button an thinkin', 'If A pick away at the cement an' plaster, A'll be able to get at the flex, pull some out an' hang mesel.' So she's

JUDY (Cont) pickin' away an' it works. Pulls a little bit o' flex. Then a bit more, an' then some more, until she's got enough ti wrap around her neck. Shouts 'Goodbye everybody! Goodbye world' and flops violently onto the floor. What happens? Anuther bloody two yard o' flex comes out the wall doesn't it? Picks herself up, and charges across the cell hopin' she might garrot hersel' on the way. More feckin' flex comes out! The cell is festooned with it. What's more all the bloody alarm bells were ringin' all over the wing. Screws dashin' around reassurin' everyone. Lookin' in the spy holes.

'Fault on the system Judy, don't worry.'

'Everythin's alright Penny, don't get upset.'

'Til they come ti the strip cell and look in. 'Nothin' ti worry about Mary. Oh my God!'

There she is, sat in the middle of all this wirin', and she's laughin'. Yes! Laughin'. The situation struck her as bein' so funny she gave up any further thought of killin' hersel'.

[*O.S. The handbell*]

[*Calling out*] Alright mam! Comin'…

[*Collecting teapot, milk jug and All-Bran. Assembling them on tray. Turning again to G.O.D.*] But here is news from the custodians of the gaols to freeze the smiles. For they report ninety young persons last year took their own lives in British prisons.

You have made a circle here 'God'. Best ya come down from that high up place and stood inside their darkness. Oh an' bring ya Commissioners. Robed in their good intention. But let them wear grey suits the better they stand like shadows. For sorrow has made holy ground of that Durham gaol where laughter would seem profane. Remembering those before us, gathered under that pale and artificial light, bones brittle with impotence. I thought I knew them but they will have changed. Only the contemptuous night to mock my sayin' 'For sixteen year I were sustained by love of you.'

JUDY (Cont) That I kept my faith in the long and witherin' hours when the darkness were about us and I were more lonely than a raven above the hills of Pennine; when there were no dawn to wake to, only the sharp distemper of remembered youth. An' I gave up thinkin' on the young fella with brown curls an' the green fields of Monaghan. An' because of my trust in your love an' carin', welcomed hysterectomy; to make a woman's gesture against her childless years.

Because you thought it fit and because you thought it right, I began the scripture class to which no one came. And because prison is where flesh meets spirit and I were the moth drawn to the light I began, at your suggestion, the poetry class where only Bridget Donachie showed up.

Poor Bridget who was not sound in her head but had a passion for me and loved my repeatin' of Yeats and the *Lake Isle of Innisfree*. And me pretendin' not ti notice when she wet herself, which she did all the time. And I said only the spiders an' birds would hear her reciting. An' that her smell reminded us of the lanes in Monaghan. Poor Bridget who begged me intercede with ya.

'I know ya talk wit 'God' Judy!'

'Will ya tell'm I were only three an'a half when A were put into care.'

'Always wonderin' where me muther an' father were.'

'An' why the' weren't lookin' for me.'

At sixteen she'd give up hope of ever knowin', and were workin' in a Glasgow Hostel run by nuns, where travellers come in for a rest and a cup o' tea, an' this day got on talkin' to an old lady. Sharin their troubles.

'Donachie? Is that your name?' The old lady asked her. And did she know an Annie Donachie? Bridget remembered a sister of that name. 'Well luv' I'm ya grandmuther.' The owld lady told her. Directin' her back to her family on a site near Manchester. But Bridget never forgive her muther. An were the only one not

JUDY (Cont) cryin' at her funeral when she died. Though the poor woman said, 'They'd declared her not to be a fit parent.' Bridget felt if her muther had really loved her she would have fought for her.

Now here she was in the same trouble.

'Judy! Help me, tell me what ti do. Me two youngest are fostered while I'm in here. And they never write. I don't know the name an' address of where they're fostered. My probation officer won't tell me. She says she can't. I love my kids, regardless of what I done. I don't want them growin' up, thinkin' about me the way I thought about my muther. 'Help me. Judy! Help me.'

[*O.S. The bell rings*]

Are ya listenin' 'God'? This is not ti plead mercy for the rejected. Or ti call on ya pity for them at the bottom o' the heap. But to cry justice for the child! Justice for those not yet born! Ti break this cycle!

[*O.S. The bell rings*]

Di ya hear me 'God'? To be declared by law unfit for ya own children. That's the cruellest thing. Nothin' compares to it. Tell ya Commissioners! Have them read Wordsworth. Like ya did me.

> Sufferin' is permanent, obscure and dark.
> And has the nature of Infinity.[6]

Tell'm study that fer sixteen year.

Sorry 'God'! Just droppin' ya in. Call it loss of faith. But I will not now come back ti Durham town. You are on ya own. Fancy tryin' a miracle? But tell ya Commissioners the interestin' quotes is scratched on the walls.

> 'The first thing ya notice in prison, after the smell.
> There is no such thing as a new day.'

Tell ya Commissioners!

---

[6] Wordsworth, W., *The Borderers, 1795-96.*

JUDY (Cont) [*O.S. The bell rings*]

Poor Bridget! In her long fight wi' the bare stone. It were the stone that won in the end. And the window high on the wall on which she stared wi' useless longin' until the night came. An' it's bars and mesh were no longer important.

[*O.S. The bell rings*]

Tell ya commissioners. These is not fit places for women an' children.

[*O.S. The bell rings*]

[*JUDY tastes the All-Bran. Recoils*] What is it about All-Bran? Puts ya in mind o' Jack Straw! [*Calling off*] Comin mam!

Answers on a postcard! Please!

[*Exit*]

THE END

Bibliography of Work

Plays, films and media work by Tom Hadaway

*Copy of publication or recording in existence.

Date	Title	Length etc.	Published Text	Performed	Broadcast
1972	*Quaker in Cullercoats*	Full length stage	No	People's Theatre	
1974	*God Bless Thee Jackie Maddison*	30 mins TV film	North Shields Libraries (2000)*		BBC TV (VHS)*
1974	*Time and Money (The Pigeon Man)*	30 minute stage	Iron Press (1999)*	Live Theatre	
1976	*The Happy Hunting Ground (Play for Today)*	Full length TV drama	No		BBC TV (VHS)*
1976	*Say Hello Say Tirra (When the Boat Comes in)*	30 minute TV drama	No		BBC TV (VHS) (2002)
1977	*The Girl Irene*	Full length stage	No	Live Theatre	
1979	*Uncle Sanghi*	30 minute TV drama	Canadian TV*		BBC TV (Schools) VHS*
1979	*May Blossoms and Fair Do's (Sea Tales)*	30 minute TV drama (narrated)	No		BBC TV *Tales of the Turning Year* (VHS)*
1983	*The Filleting Machine*	30 minute TV and stage	Iron Press (and others)*	Live Theatre and others	Channel 4

Date	Title	Length etc.	Published Text	Performed	Broadcast
1984	*The Low Street*	Full length stage and TV drama	No	Live Theatre	BBC2
1985	*Alice and Yussuf*	Drama for stage	No	Live Theatre	
1986	*Sea Coal*	Feature Film	No		Amber Films (VHS)*
1986	*The Long Line*	3 part drama (stage)	Iron Press*	Live Theatre	
1987	*Yesterday's Children*	Full length drama stage	University of Sunderland Press* (2004)	Live Theatre	
1988	*The Prison Writer*	Full Length Radio drama	No		BBC Radio 4
1988	*For the Love of Two Boys*	30 minute radio drama	No		BBC Radio 4
1989	*In Fading Light*	Feature film	No		Amber Films VHS*
1991	*Long Shadows (co-written with Pauline Hadaway)*	Full length stage	University of Sunderland Press* (2004)	Live Theatre	Extracts-Tyne Tees TV (VHS)*
1993	*Sea Farers*	2 part drama (stage)	North Shields Library*	Live Theatre	
1997	*Let the Child Sing*	30 minute stage	No	Live Theatre	
1997	*Falling Together (co-written with Pauline Hadaway)*	Full length stage	No	Live Theatre	

Date	Title	Length etc.	Published Text	Performed	Broadcast
1999	*The Vicious Circle*	30 minute stage	University of Sunderland Press* (2004)	Big Mama Productions	
2000	*Postcard from God*	30 minute stage	University of Sunderland Press* (2004)	Live Theatre	
2004	*Laurel and Hardy*	Full length stage	No	Work in progress	